1

Astrology made Simple:

A Beginners Approach

Antoinette E. M. John

Reading At Its Best
P.O Box 1366
Roswell, GA 30076

Phone: 678-793-5528

First published by Reading At Its Best

Library of Congress Control Number: 2013919172

ISBN 978-1987768176
ISBN 1987768175
 All scriptures were taken from the bible, Kings James, New King James, and The Message Bible.

Contents

Introduction:

In the early years, astrology was used as a tool to deliver a deeper sense of wisdom for the human development, which was both collective and significant. "Astrology is a science because it is fundamentally mathematical." (Goldstein-Jacobson, 1975 p. 24) However, it gives concrete apparatuses for allocating change and its proper timing. The archetypal ideas help to build a solid foundation within astrology, and can be applied to every individual's life. This divine idea is embodied in an expression that gives a clear and detailed picture of an individual's destiny. Typically, astrology is influenced by different factors, which contributes to the state of mankind, and the environment which it governs: the solar system helps to depict one's life journey, from the time of birth.

It is one of the greatest adventures of the human civilization, and of course, it has contributed to the human experience. The purpose of astrology is to use the positions of the planets and stars in the sky to gather information on the individual. Astrology is a system that enables us to understand the past, present, and the future. Also, it is an idea that encompasses the ideal of a structured body of knowledge of the cosmos, along with the way in, which the stars give meaning to our lives. It gives us the ability to explore ourselves, our relationships and our place in the world.

Furthermore, this can be set as a map to human destiny. "Astrology was almost certainly developed originally by man as a result of his earliest experience of the fact, while the mist-enveloped, hot, damp jungle where primitive man lived brought to him constantly unexpected life-or-death encounters, the clear skies." (Rudhyar, 1980 p. 25) An astrologer will draw up a chart, in order to understand how the events have an influence on relationships and the individual. The chart will be filled with mysterious symbols, which is a snapshot of the cosmic heavenlies, and secrets will be expressed to show the human behavior.

However, these symbols will give deep meaning to things that are not visible to the naked eye. Astrology is an incredible tool of self-discovery. It helps to bring all the pieces of the puzzle together, in someone's life. It can also shed light on any inner conflictions and contradictions that may be harboring in someone's subconscious mind. It never stops revealing new layers of thought, because it can be used as a map to understand the psyche. There is also chemistry to astrology which helps the individual, by providing clues as to why he or she is attracted to or are indifferent to those that they meet.

Furthermore, astrology helps you to better understand how to formulate and apprehend your relationships, whether it is with a spouse, parents, siblings, bosses, co-workers, friends, and business partners. This can be done by comparing birth charts, which will alert you of any area of conflict; and would show you where karma is being played out. All this really comes from energy fields of the individual. "Human beings are functioning energy fields; we're composites of many energy fields that are functioning simultaneously in an inter-related way." (Arroyo, 1993 p. 80) The energy fields are activated in relationships, and they would be detected in the charts of the individuals.

"The time of conception is not a matter of chance. It is the self-ordained creative basis of physical form leading to birth and it does not take place in the same given time in general following population." (Goldstein-Jacobson, 1975, p. 9) Astrology has to do with the art of studying relationships between people and events on earth and the cycles. How the planets corresponds with each other, and how they move along the ecliptic. The ancient art of astrology was introduced to ancient Rome around the second B.C. which was incorporated in the Roman religion. The high priest sought the advice of the astrologers, before making any major decisions and this was the most popular technique used in Rome.

Furthermore, during the Roman Empire, astrology was used as an important tool in politics, which of course, it was used to predict the end of one cycle, and the beginning of a new era. It is also known for depicting the energies of the solar system and how it affects us, as humans, and it even gives deeper insights in making the right choices.

In fact, there is more to astrology, and it is deeper and more meaningful than the horoscope. The path of a person's life is, ultimately, the sum total of his/her aura from previous birth lives. There are several forms of astrology, which are: Western, Vedic or Jyotish, and Chinese. Vedic and Jyotish astrology deals with mathematical calculations of the planets and constellations when they are in motion and give details and predictions of the future. They are practiced mostly by Indian astrologers from early ancient days. The ancient language that was used was Sanskrit and according to the dictionary, it means "an ancient indic language that is the language of Hinduism and the Vedas and the classical literary language of India." It was used by the highly educated class and for religious purposes.

Practicing this form of astrology bears significance to the Hindu culture, especially when they are about to name a child. Western astrology; however, shares some of the characteristics as that of Vedic and Jyotish, but differs in the way how the zodiac is measured. In Western astrology, the gesticulations of the planets are measured alongside the position of the Sun. The aspirations and insights of this method start from the first sign of the zodiac, Aries, at the time of spring equinox. The science of astrology precedes other sciences, including politics and even religion. It has a great influence on the Greeks, the Romans, the Chinese, and the Egyptians. It is believed that the planets telegraph their efforts and energies to us via charismatic signals, which are perceived by neural network, beginning in the womb.

Consequently, the image that is formed in the neural network of the child, at the time of birth, is influenced by types of signs and this causes the individual to respond differently. "The moment of conception starts the beginning of the body, the vehicle being prepared for the occupancy for the soul-in-waiting." (Goldstein-Jacobson, 1975 p. 9)

In Hindu astrology, also known as Vedic or Jyotish astrology, an ancient Indian, which has three branches. This is used to give information about events, such as wars, political events, and earthquakes. The foundation is based on the Vedas (scriptures) and there is a connection with the microcosm and macrocosm. The procedures are differently from that of the western astrology (Hellenistic). There are numerous sub-systems of interpretation and calculation with the elements that are not found in Hellenistic astrology. This is an important facet in the lives of many Hindus. Many of them consult the stars, before making a decision about marriage, opening a business, moving into a new home, and before naming a child.

14

Their charts are a lot differently to that of western astrology. This is a chart used in North India

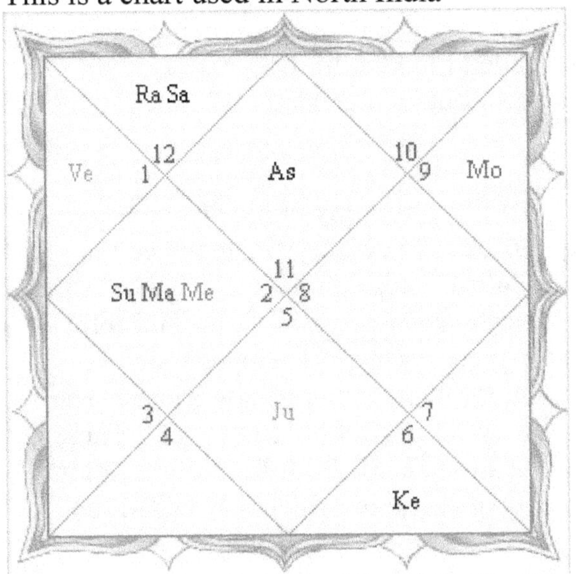

This is a chart used in South India:

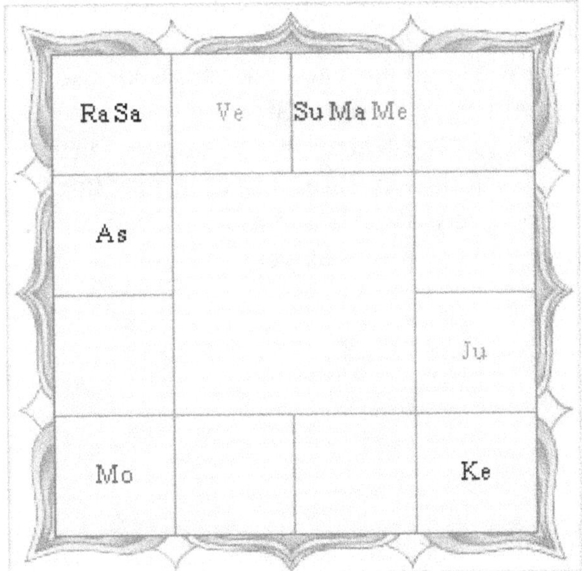

They are divided into twelve equal parts on an imaginary belt of 360 degrees, which is called a sign or a rasi. However, the planets are consistent with the actual zodiac, as oppose to western astrology, which the planets fall within the signs.

15

The natal chart is called the bhava chakra and it is a complete 360 degrees circle of life. The planets that are ruling the trines are called the Dasha, and the primary system that is used is the Vimshottari dasha system, which is used to measure the natal Moon. Additionally, each dasha is divided into sub periods called bhuktis. In the Vedic system, there is a simpler house system that is used, but all signs are associated with only one house.

Chinese astrology is tied in with astronomy, which came to flourish during the Han Dynasty (around 2nd century BC to 2nd century AD). There is a close relationship with Chinese philosophy (which is the theory of three harmony, heaven, earth, and water), but it has different principles to that of western astrology. A person's destiny can be determined by the position of the major planets in a person's chart. The position of the Sun and Moon has a direct impact on this as well. There is; however, a system of twelve animal signs that is built from observations of the orbit. This is divided into twelve sections, which is rounded to twelve years.

Their method of finding the masculine and feminine is, when the years end in an even number, it is Yang and the year that ends with an uneven number is Yin. The twelve different animal signs represent twelve different personalities. Their system can be used to calculate someone's fate and destiny, based on the individual's birthday, birth hour and birth season. It is considered that the stars in the sky form basis for fairy tales. One of the beliefs of the Chinese people is that; if an individual is born in January, that person can have a sign of the previous year.

The Sun Signs:

Hence, there are twelve signs in the zodiac, which is an important and critical step, so that it can give a clear degree of accuracy. If the Sun signs are used with the wrong attitude, it can be misleading. It provides a reliable method of how to analyze people, and how to better understand human nature. Also, it gives comprehensive information, which can be approximately 80% accurate. The Suns signs are located the moment an individual takes his or her first breath, and this is the exact position taken from the ephremeris. However, if someone is born on the first or the last day of a Sun sign, the exact time of birth must be calculated, including the place of birth in order to know if the sun changed signs.

Furthermore, the names of the Sun signs are: Aries, Taurus, Gemini, Cancer, Leo, Virgo, Libra Scorpio, Sagittarius, Capricorn, Aquarius, and Pisces. Additionally, they are divided "into twelve 30o sectors. They indicate in which sector the Sun was found at the time of your birth. The zodiac most commonly used in Western astrology is determined by the vernal equinox. This is the position of the Sun (about March 20 of each year)." (Sakoian & Acker, 2001 p. 3)

Aries:

Aries is considered to be the spring equinox, and it is the beginning of the zodiac year. It represents the Ram and is very adventurous, which brings out ambitions as one of the qualities, and it gives way to impulsivity in the individual. It is conscious of the self, and can be absorbed with his needs. It is the infant, and can be a bit selfish, and the individual who is an Arian will call someone at early hours in the morning, because he or she wants to get something off of their mind, without thinking about the other person.

It is impossible to resist an individual who is an Aries because their smile shall draw many people to them: since there is a sense of innocence about the individual. Arians may be a bit hesitant to submit to instructions if the person disagrees. Arians look at themselves in a new way; however, one would be motivated in any cause that is interesting to the individual.

17

"However their impulsiveness and ability to listen to the advice of others tend to involve them in difficulties. Since they are highly competitive, Arians seek to be the first and best in whatever they do. Arians need to learn the lesson of lesson, so that they can relate to offers and reach out to them with consideration." (Sakoian & Acker, 2001 p. 34)

As an Arian you are a natural born leader, but you may not be very effective at completing tasks. You would not shy away from new ground, and Arians are normally call "the pioneers of the zodiac", and are considered to be fearless. Aries is the symbol of the Ram, and it is a Cardinal fire sign which is both good and bad, due to the impulsiveness of the individuals who are ruled by this sign. However, as an Arian you may be tempted to ram your ideas down everyone's throat without thinking about asking them, it they are interested in knowing about them. Aries is ruled by Mars, which is the God of war. This is where you naturally get the fearless abilities from, and you would not be afraid of any battle, which is an important key to the courage and the aggressiveness of the individuals ruled by Aries.

Furthermore, as an Arian, you may tend to think about the self, and may lack the sense of stability. "It is an energy of ego drive saying "I want to become what I am", but it is not yet what could be. It is willful, but the will is not stabilized. Its intention can change rapidly." (Hand 1981 p. 211)
You live in the moment, and may not take things seriously. It is important that, as an Arian, you learn how to adjust to the needs of others, but this is not always fulfilled. Individuality is of importance, and you tend to isolate yourself from others, and avoid confrontation. Arians desires to take control over the self and not over others and at times: can be antisocial; however Aries loves to have his or her own way. One of the ultimate goals for Aries is to express the self and has little concern for time, or if it is practical. Interestingly, Aries can think in the abstract and of course, it must reflect the hidden desires. It is easier for you to reveal more energy rather than taking it in, because it shows how much of a talker you are and lacks the discipline to listen.

Patience is not one of Aries fortitude, and it lacks the diligence to complete things; and may also lack the emotional balance, but is strong in showing enthusiasm, confidence and anger. However, Aries does not hold on to anger, once it comes out, it is easily forgotten, and is not too quick to cooperate by acting in a false manner. It is important for Aries to represent themselves in a Positive manner.

The Sun in Aries:

When the Sun is in Aries, you will have a strong desire to be recognized, especially in terms of work that is done by you. This brings out the winning and competitive edge in you. Aries "tries to fill the need for recognition with self-assertion and direct competitive actions. Forceful assertion of individuality is necessary for full self-expression." (Arroyo, 1989 p. 52) You love to be seen, and can be the center of attraction in a gathering. Independence is very important to you, and you will speak your mind, whether people like it or not. You believe in yourself and in your abilities.

It can be impossible for an Arian to tolerate the opinion of others, especially when they are opposing your ideas which you would think are always right. People with the Sun in Aries tend to be quick and direct, and they would react without thinking things through. It is easy to see what you want, and go for it. In essence, you can put pressure on yourself, because you have an inherent feeling of perfection. Energy level is high, and you do things quickly; for example, walking and getting dressed. You possess a temper, but do not harbor ill feelings, nor hold grudges. With Aries as your Sun sign you may find that it is easier for you to have complaints about headaches, problems with the eyes, and with the sinus.

However, there may also be some problems with minor rashes on the skin, but this is not always likely. When the Sun is in Aries people love to smile, and possess the role as being very independent, early in life. They do not run to others for help, because they love to do things for themselves. It is easy to hide true feelings from others mostly when meeting new people.

The Moon in Aries:

When the Moon is in Aries you can react in a hostile and impatient manner. You love new things, and want to bring your inner thoughts into your experience. "A confident action-oriented sense of self focused on new experience. Responds to experience and environment with a single-pointed release of energy. Combative qualities can hinder attainment of security." (Arroyo 1989 p. 57) It is important to have instant gratification.

You are adventurous and it can be difficult for you to settle down to daily routine. Aries are passionate about people and the things that they are doing. It is not easy to commit to long term projects because you tend to feel trapped.

Aries crave to be the master of their own success but can blame their failure on others, quickly. It is easy for Arians to become self-indulgent and over confident in themselves. Women with their moon in Aries can be aggressive in romance and other situations which require a delicate approach. But, they are emotionally suited to conquer challenges that many people cannot endure. On the other hand, men with their Moon in Aries expect too much and give little in romance, but they tend to have an original approach in life. Arians can be affected in different ways, especially when it comes to following through on projects that they have started. You tend to get bored very easily, when the action stops. Bringing up past events is not a good idea to do with Arians, since they do not recall things that have happened moments ago.

Taurus:

However, Taurus is a fixed earth sign, and you tend to be set in your ways. Change is not a pursuit that is confortable, because you do not like change. This Sun sign is considered a negative introvert sign that loves reward. Also, as a Taurean, you love physical pleasures and material goods. Likes beautiful things, and loves to look beautiful and is very sensitive to the touch. You love a good meal, along with fine wine. Taurus loves to live the good life, and also love arts and craft. There is an artistic side to people who are ruled by this sign. You can be very stubborn, and loves your own way and want to get things done in a timely manner. Persistency is one of the traits that usually show up in the personality of people who are ruled by this sign. Pursuing your goals is very important, and you are reliable and people can count on you.

You are not afraid of hard work, and of course you can be a bit self- indulgent. You seek to give yourself luxurious things and would not deny yourself anything. Pleasing yourself is a lifelong dream. Beautifying the home with your creative art and home décor brings out the inner charm in you, especially when you are entertaining. You may also be misunderstood by others, and people may think that you are materialistic. You strive for a happy home life and yearn for a stable relationship. The element of peace and harmony is associated with the life style that you seek to live. You are a conformist and of course, this can be seen in your day to day behavior. You will work hard to make your mate happy, so that peace can be a part of your home.

Since the Bull is the symbol for Taurus, you tend to be a bit possessive, when it comes to your mate. Taureans are romantic to the core, and they are also loyal to the people they hold close to their heart. You tend to take things slowly, until you get to your goals. You may be a bit argumentative, due to your somewhat short temper, but you can calm down and forget about what caused the argument in the first place, due to the earth that is a part of the sign. You value family and friends, and at times, will do anything for them. You have a lot of energy and would need to do outdoor activities to burn it off. Also, Taurus loves to do things that would keep them centered and close to earth. It is important to always keep the neck warm during the winter, since Taurus rules the neck and throat. The best color for this should be earth tone. Taurus do not mind being by itself, and does not have to be too sociable, and does not need the approval of others.

"Taurus is earthy in the popular meaning of the word: it enjoys the physical world. It sees the physical universe as neither an arena in which to perform nor as a tool. Rather, it wants to be a part of, involved in, and especially to experience the wonder of the physical world." (Hand, 1989 p. 213-214)

Sun in Taurus:

When the Sun in Taurus, it shows that you tend to be down to earth. You can display a deep sense of sensuality, in whatever you do. Yes you are more rooted in the physical world that the other signs and you can be unmovable and unstoppable. Taurus does not take risk into anything, but stands firm on the decisions that are made. You do not give up on your goals that easily, even if others give up. You are a natural builder, and would want to see the plans of any project before moving forward. You are dependable and once you are in charge, everything will go the way that it is planned. You are in it for the long haul, and you would not quit, until the project is done right.

When the Sun is in Taurus, you can be easy going, but when you get mad, a raging Bull comes to the scene. However, you can establish order by force. "Forceful assertion of individuality is necessary for full self-expression. Identifies self as explorer, pioneer, the first to begin an adventure; quickly grasps essentials." (Arroyo 1989 p. 52)

The Moon in Taurus:

With the Moon in Taurus, you love familiarity, which is an important aspect to daily routine which of course, contributes to your strong will. You depend on your senses to feel and you are rooted in your ways. It is important that you feel safe and content, especially in the home. Taureans do not like to be pushed into doing anything. The strong effects of the Moon contribute to this. You will go out of your way to avoid confrontations that will cause emotional outbursts. It may be a bit difficult for Taurus to understand the need for their mate to grow, change, or to want emotional stimulation. With the Moon in this sign you are generally very romantic, and your affections are very strong, deep, and steadfast. Protecting yourself and your interests is very important to you. In fact, Taureans will hardly make a move without deciding that it is safe, and there is something in it for them.

When the Moon is in Taurus, people normally have reliable instincts, and they tend to have a good sense of smell. When one is in a relationship with people who are born with the Moon in this position, it can be quite enduring and fulfilling. Taureans tend to hang on to their mate, even if there is conflict in the relationship, and break ups do not happen easily. They do not adapt easily, especially when their routine is interrupted. Spontaneity is not one of their strong holds. This eliminates the element of surprise. Taurus "reacts slowly to any experience; maintains stability and poised when faced with other demands. Flows into physical sensations emotionally retaining the feeling of touching and savoring the pleasure of the moment. (Arroyo, 1989 p. 57)

Gemini:

Gemini is a mutable sign that represents communication and often: you will love to talk and express yourself. However, it is not just idle chatter, but they love to speak about events and thought provoking conversations; which is considered to be a part of their mind. It is natural for you to be intellectually inclined, and you will find yourself probing places and people in search of information. After the information is gathered, it is important to Gemini to share it with people, and the more information that is collected the better, and it is a lot of fun collecting and sharing it. Gemini's are extremely very interested in developing their relationships, and involvements with these folks are enjoyable. "Like the wind the nature of Gemini is to move rapidly from place to place, covering it what it encounters. It learns quickly but does not develop that deep feeling understanding of the word that enables some people to live skillfully without having to think." (Hand, 1981 p. 216)

Interestingly, Gemini's are the life of the party and is known to be bright and quick witted. It is easy for you to rationalize and this can be done effortlessly, and it is easy to use your imagination. It is very easy to balance both sides of any situation and issues. At times, you may be considered to be restless or indecisive, which is due to the fact that you do not know which one of the twins will show up. Gemini's are flexible, and it is easy to go with the flow, which of course is the reason why you are so adaptable. Indeed, you are a multi tasker. This is a good thing when you consider the innumerable interest that accompanies it, because this sign is a mutable sign, and it is easy to think and process thoughts.

People ruled by the sign of Gemini are clever and curious, and are normally the hit at a cocktail party. They also love to listen and learn. It is important to be around stimulating people who can add to thought provoking conversations, because you will get bored, if you don't. At social settings, it is easy for you to be charming and good natured, because you love to share yourself with your friends. Because Gemini lack reserve about the way they do things, some people may take this as being misconstrued and scheming, but their hearts are normally in the right place. One thing you would not do is disappoint others. It is also easy to look at projects from more than one side, and can come up with logical ideas.

Evidently, this makes a Gemini a valuable asset to any team. Making connections is an important aspect to Gemini and would do it their way. There is lightness to your spirit and you have a youthful energy that helps you to appear forever young. You are always ready to play, due to your youthful energy. You will also love being a part of a book club, because it will help to stimulate your mind. Deep breathing and meditating is important to do, since Gemini rules the lungs. "Gemini is usually quite sociable, and enjoys meeting people. The sign has a fairly high energy level which other people find refreshing, yet the level is not as exhausting to those of a slower temperament." (Hand, 1981 p. 216)

The Sun in Gemini

However, with the Sun in Gemini, your personality can be hard to describe, since it tends to change, all the time. Gemini voracious curiosities usually help them to learn new things, which of course, can make some of them walking encyclopedias, full of knowledge and wisdom. One of the things that can be attached to your personality is the laughter that can be heard, before you see a Gemini. You have a deep interest in people and often times can be called the peace maker. It is not easy to pin you down, but you will make an excellent friend. This can also be integrated in a relationship, especially when you need to communicate with your mate. The perfect companion for a Gemini is someone who thinks on the same level, so that you would not be tied up in one dull topic.

It is important that you maintain the space to grow, and you would not want anyone to hold you down, or hinder you from growing. Gemini loves to explore the world, at will, because it is full of fascination. You will prove your loyalty in a relationship in time, but you are very loyal and faithful. Gemini needs to make over the self many times, so that they can follow every thread of inspiration. They may appear to be restless, at times, and may be considered to be a bit inconsistent or flaky. Once a Gemini finds a topic that is worthy of their colorful mind, a deeper mastery can be sought and achieved. You are a natural born charmer, and most often, you can wear a grin symbolizing that all is well, and it is ok to take a risk. Gemini has "creative energy directed toward perception acquiring facts, asking questions, and toward finding connections between ideas. Needs to express self verbally and to receive recognition for intellectual abilities." (Arroyo, 1989 p. 52)

The Moon in Gemini:

People with the Moon in Gemini normally have brightly lit up minds, and they are always thinking and creating. There is always an interesting topic to interact, talk about and lean. Indeed, this brings out the social butterfly of the crowd. You are a good listener, and are intrigued by the human condition. When the Moon is in Gemini, it can be a bit difficult for you to relax, and when you are winding down, you will have different conduits receiving information at one time, such as TV, radio and surfing the net. You are intrigued with technology, and can find many ways to use it to your advantage. There is a need for stimulation, because the world would benefit from your gifts. Many Gemini's are fine writers, artists, or even comedians, because they are in tuned with their surroundings.

Gemini in romance is an enchanting mate, and is a fun and loving individual, and would love a mate who possess an adaptable outlook, so that your nervous temperament can be soothed. In a relationship with a Gemini, it is easy and fresh and evolving, because you love variety. You tend to read a lot and think on insightful things. Home improvement and reorganizing and beautifying it keep them happy. You are normally bored with routine and constancy. When you have plenty things to do, you are at your best. Gemini has a way with words, and is clear and witty. Your imagination is boundless. It is not a good idea to irritate a Gemini, because they can be moody. You love to talk things out to find common ground. There is a need for them to get in touch with their own feelings.

Cancer:

Cancer is Cardinal water sign and loves to move about in life in a rhetorical manner. You are very protective of yourself, and would retrieve when you are hurt. Cancerians are very sensitive, but they are able to resist changes in an environment, which can help to protect themselves from unfriendly environments. You can be on the defensive, because you are emotional and you try very hard to hide it. You love family and is nurturing towards those you hold dearly. "It does so by putting one back in contact with one's source, one's roots. Cancer is not merely feeling; it is a feeling part of something. Cancer is an emotional awareness, one that can be inchoate." (Hand, 1989 p. 218) Your nature to appreciate the home and family give you the ability to create a secure home; one that you can retire to and feel safe. Your desire is not to impress others about your home, but you want a place to exercise your maternal instincts.

Cancer is not considered to be unsociable, because they believe that there is a time to socialize and a time to be solitary. You tend to have a strong intuition and can identify with situation with others, due to your imagination. It is easy to sympathize with others, especially those you love. You are artistic, and possess intellectual abilities. In fact, you can make an excellent actor/actress, and you have great leadership skills with the youths. In personal relationships, you can exhibit both softness and a tough demeanor, and you are very romantic and can have sentimental fantasies, but in a marriage, you are loyal. Cancer thinks of themselves as the protector in families. You give much and ask for little in return. Cancerians have a great memory, especially when it deals with their emotions. The body part that is ruled by this sign is the breast and this relates to their deep emotional side.

One of Cancer functional abilities is that you are able to do various amount of occupations. You are very much interested in what people think and feel. Some of the occupations that you can function well in is journalism, writing, or in politics, and public affairs, for example, welfare or nursing. You are a lover of antiques, because "Cancer symbolizes the need for emotional security, for feeling that one's environment will support one's existence, and for feeling nurtured by those around one." (Hand, 1981 p. 218)

The Sun in Cancer:

One would develop a strong survival instinct, and you are protective of those you love. You love to share your deep inner feelings with the world and love to reminisce about past events. You can be moody, and you can be misunderstood by others. Cancer needs roots because you can resist change. You want to feel secure and safe in everything you do. With the Sun in Cancer, you do not always like it when people are blunt with you, and you create a thick shell, so that you would not be hurt by others. This can cause you to withdraw into a retreat all by yourself. You tend to shine best when you are focused on others and you are trying to fix their problems. You use this as a defense, so that you would not get hurt.

Cancer can solve problems with ease, but you worry and cling to others too much. Teaching kids or running a daycare is a natural ability. You are naturally attracted to caring professions, such as: social work, counseling, psychology, nursing, and teaching. You are a natural cook, and you would enjoy working from home and anything in medicine. You tend to show a gentle and kind heart towards others, unless you are hurt, and then everyone would know. "Experiences strength through nurturing, sensitive, mother like qualities. Feels instinctive urge to protect one's ego; builds inner self a nest from which it can safely radiate. Sense of individuality is expressed most clearly in a familiar sheltered environment or situation." (Arroyo, 1989 p.53)

Moon in Cancer:

The Moon is at home in this sign, since it rules it. It is easy for you to get in touch with the feelings of others. Your memory of the past is impeccable, especially relating to things that are emotionally attached to you. It is easy for you to attach yourself to things, and cling to the people that you love. It is important to seek security in everything that you do and you naturally love peace and quiet. You are a devoted individual, and you are loyal to your spouse. One of the most important things is: you do not like to be taken for granted, and you do not like confrontations. The Moon in this water sign shows that you do not like boundaries, and can maneuver your way around obstacles. You have a good sense of humor. People mostly appreciate your unique outlook on life.

Cancer would return the favor when they are treated with kindness. You love to succeed, because this helps to put you in a good mood. Normally, you are dependable, despite your mood swings, which can be displayed, occasionally. Cancer can be over sensitive, at times. You feel a sense of security when you are nurturing others. You can be "extremely sensitive too moods and reactions strong memory of past emotions is retained forever, still coloring attitudes toward present situations." (Arroyo, 1989 p. 58)

Leo:

Leos love to make an impression on people that they come in contact with, and people are drawn to them. On the other hand, Leo is a sign that loves to be in the spot light, and it is impossible to miss you, because you love being the center of attraction. You are very ambitious, and it is easy for you to accomplish your goals, once you put your mind to it. Also, you are creative and it is fun for you to do your projects. It is also easy for you to be in the limelight. Leo is dramatic, and your flair for drama can land you in Hollywood. You are warm and enthusiastic since this is part of your core, and it is a pleasure to be around you. You also love pleasure. Because of your self-confidence, you think that you are the ruler of the Universe. "With Leo, the basic structure of the individual entity is complete. This is clear in that Leo is a sign of developed ego and self-confidence, with the strong needs for self-expression, admiration, and uncompromising personal integrity." (Hand, 1981 p. 219) Leo is fascinated with the self, and can be a bit self-indulgent.

You are very distinguished and strong, and like the Lion: you get things done. When you are a member on a team, you are reliable to get things done, because you see things to completion. At times, you can be a bit overbearing and domineering. This is due to the ruler of the sign, which is the Sun and fixed fire quality. The Sun is fixed and does not move, and this makes Leos set in their ways, making them a bit impossible to deal with, because once they make up their mind, it is hard to persuade them. You can be a well-organized individual, and it is easy for you to inspire others. You think that you are the key and main ingredient to everything, and if anyone tells you differently, he or she would have to watch out. You are an outgoing individual and have the zest for life. You are antisocial. There is a principle to Leo, which is being like a child who has achieved something new, yet not happy until everyone knows about it.

There is a significant "need for personal recognition, a desire to be impressive and a need to control one's destiny. The desire to be impressive is usually a desire to genuinely so-that is to be an individual of real significance not merely to appear significant." (Hand, 1981 p. 220)

You have a generous spirit and of course, you feel the need to succeed, which may come across being bossy, but this would not detour you from your path in life. Leos are loyal and love to receive honor. You are decisive and are very romantic. You are fearless, and you do not commit to failure, nor do you accept failure. Naturally, you are warm hearted, and you want to make sure that everyone is happy. You are great at handling money, and you are sought after by friends and family. Your needs are clearly defined, you would take things to heart. Since Leo rules the heart you would have to take deep breaths and slow down. You strive to be acknowledged by others, but you are very independent. "Leo's only real dependency upon others is that it badly needs their acknowledgement." (Hand 1981 p. 220)

The Sun in Leo:

When the Sun is in Leo, you are considered to be untamed and it is a bit difficult to translate you. It is not easy for you to blend in. There is a dominating force about you, and a need to fulfill your heart's desires. In this sign, Leo, the Sun is most radiant, because it is the planet that rules it. Leo is both fiery and impulsive with a stubborn streak. You need to express yourself in an absolute way. Being on the stage will help you to release some of your energy, and you love being the star, director or writer. There is an inner need to dominate and control your circumstances. You are a visionary, and you are receptive when it comes to going with the flow. You are brilliant and different; you want to be you. It is likely that you can be easily hurt.

Leos are broad minded, expansive, faithful, and loving, which makes you ambitious; and you want a career that needs organization and creativity. You will make an excellent employer. You do love luxury in every sense. Leo loves the good things in life, and you are friendly and flamboyant, but you stand firm in your beliefs. A woman who is a Leo is outspoken and forthright and you leave nothing to mystery. She loves people to flatter her, and seeks to receive romance as her fortitude. Because of her bold confidence, she will hold the position of CEO with ease. In marriage, she would not consider herself being a housewife, nor would she want to stay home, unless she runs a business there.

As a woman, you are not just a mother, but you are a career oriented individual with hobbies and passions. She rules her children with in a warm dominant manner. A man who is a Leo loves being on center stage, and does not like to follow orders, because he would not be the best that he can be. It can be a bit impossible not to like him, because he is warm, friendly, outgoing, and loves to have fun. Children loves him, due to the magic that he has. He is a natural born leader, and attracts people like a magnet. When he makes a commitment, he will never let go. As a Leo, you are "motivated by a need to be recognized for one's generosity. Radiates confidence and encouragement to others; can visualize and enterprise. Pride is a dominant personality characteristic; heartfelt but childlike emotions are always at work." (Arroyo, 1981 p. 53)

Moon in Leo:

With the Moon in Leo, you attribute a lot to entertaining at home, and of course: you have a great sense of humor. You are talented and make an excellent organizer, but you would also want to control your friends. Deep within: you want to treat others fairly. You need a lot of love and support, and you can get dramatic when you feel as though you are being slighted. You tend to suppress your feelings, and you hurt by yourself, preferably at home. To you, social status is important, so you are less likely to make a scene in public. Leo's exaggerate a lot, because of self-expression. You don't like it when people are ungrateful, because you express your gratitude openly. You have a lot of pride, which is your own down fall, and you tend to possess an ego, which allow you to take charge of everything. Ultimately, you are attached to power. Once you believe in a cause, you will make the sacrifice.

In personal relationships, you can be the possessive jealous type, and if there is a break up your ego feels the pain more than the other person. With the Moon in this sign, Leo can be very artistic and you will love the arts to fuel your artistic abilities. You are not a risk taker, and you love to feel safe tucked away in your comfort zone. It is important that you do not fail in the presence of others. You do not take advice well, but you are always happy to give it. You have the feelings that you are always right, and don't want anyone to tell you what to do. Leo "puts much creative energy into the environment and can be supportive and encouraging towards others. Adapt to life by dramatizing, creating new situations, using humor to entertain others." (Arroyo, 1981 p. 58)

Virgo:

The sixth sign of the zodiac is Virgo, and people who are born under this sign can be very humorous. Being picky is something that comes natural with them. As a Virgo you tend to pay attention to details, but this is for a reason, and that is to help others. You were born to serve, and you do this with great joy. You are logical, and because of this: you are very efficient. It is important to you that you work for the greater good. Indeed you are an asset in the work place, because you are dependable, and you can get things done, the first time. Virgos are balanced and fair when they are assessing everyone. You must, at all times, keep yourself busy: because you are not the one to sit still. There is a combination of mental and physical energy that you have. You are considered to be very intelligent.

You are a natural communicator, and you can utilize your mental acuity to your advantage. Virgo would study every situation in great detail, so that you would be able to analyze it carefully. It is imperative that you understand everything. You are a perfectionist, but will not admit it, which is why you are so neat and clean. Being reliable and practical is an asset as to why people would want you around. Virgo is a mutable earth, which is why you are so grounded. You are humble and easy going, which is something that you prefer, anyway. Enjoying material possession is something that you like, even if you would not admit it, and you are very picky of whom you bring into your life. You are very health conscious, and you would have loads of information on diet and hygiene. Being in the health field will help to stimulate your senses.

In love and romance, Virgo is dedicated to their lovers, and they can be a bit jealous, at times. You are an essential helpmate. "Virgo approaches the physical universe as an obstacle to which one must adapt, a frame working through which one can learn to be effective, and a reality that must be served." (Hand, 1981 p. 222) Service and loyalty is very important to you, and you do not have a problem being submissive. Getting along with your peers are very important to Virgo, and you are capable of making the best of it. You do not look for recognition when doing a job, but for the quality of the job that you are doing: making sure that it is well done. This is why you do not need the approval of others to know that you are doing a great job. Virgo do not feel the need to be treated like royalty, but solely wants to be accepted for the self and who you are as an individual.

Sun in Virgo:

When the Sun is in Virgo, people tend to have good mannerisms, and they are very practical about their appearance. There is an amazing aura about you and people see it, and loves you because of it. You are sensitive and aware of your body image, and if you do not like what you see, you can be a bit uncomfortable with it. Being attracted to mind and body is essential to you, and meditating helps to bring balance to your spiritual life. You are particular about food, and can have a good appetite, but you are picky about food and what you put into your body. Virgo can have the tendency to worry a lot, especially when you have been faced with new situations, because you notice the intriguing details.

As a result, you tend to attract people who need help. There is a beautiful charm to Virgo, and people find this irresistible. You have a lot to offer, and you will help a friend to get out of a jam. It is easy for you to develop specialized skills and techniques in a very practical manner. Virgo is usually "motivated by need to be helpful to be a service in a tangible way. Radiates intelligence and clean-edged vitality. Attunement to soul values, and constant need to improve oneself." (Arroyo, 1989 p. 54)

Moon in Virgo:

31

Being perfect is something that needs to be managed by Virgo, because you are very critical, mostly of the self. If you are not careful, you may encounter self-esteem problems. You are a very private person, and do not like to discuss your personal business with just anyone. It is important to give yourself credit for a job well done. You can have an impeccable memory, and this may annoy many people, because you will remember things in great detail. Virgo loves animals, because they would not criticize them. You work well with your hands, and loves crafts, and you will make a great musician. This way, you can express yourself in your music.

Furthermore, if you are not happy on your job or career, you may encounter stress, and will be a bit difficult to live in an environment where there is chaos. Taking care of your possessions is something that you take seriously, and you will have a fit if anyone harms it in any way. Virgos have a concern for health and how they treat their bodies. Also, you are the one to make sure that you take your vitamins and minerals, and eat natural or organic food. You are also very practical with the way that you respond to everything and everyone. Virgo "responds analytically to all experiences; needs a sense of order in the environment to feel comfortable. Refines emotional reactions in order to perfect their expression." (Arroyo, 1989 p. 59)

Libra:

Balance is what best describes this sun sign. It is the seventh sign of the zodiac. Libra is represented by the scale, and it is the only inanimate sign, which is considered the most reliable sign in the zodiac: because it represents the zenith of the year. Librans are considered to be the most civilized of all the sun signs. You have elegance, charm, and good taste. You are naturally kind, gentle, and love beauty and harmony. One of your gifts is your critical faculty, and how you are able to look at matters, from an impartial judgment. Librans would make good lawyers and judges. When you get to a conclusion, you do not tolerate argument from anyone. You are sensitive to the needs of others and you know how to connect with your intuitions. You know how to make everyone feel better. Librans are very sociable individuals, and they do not like it when others are treated unfair, nor do they like conflict.

"So it is with Libra. Though it is the sign in which the individual first makes an accommodation to another individual in a one-to-one relationship." (Hand, 1981 p. 225) You have more of an artistic, rather than the intellectual mind. It is easy for you to observe people, because your critical abilities are fueled by your perceptions. In personal relationships, Librans know how to show understanding of their spouse's opinion, and it is important to you to resolve any differences in a compromising manner. And, in most cases, you will settle any differences to your disadvantage, just to save the relationship. You love the opposite sex, and may fantasize about them. When in marriage, there is a good chance for success, because Librans are well known to be the union of the three minds, and their kindness to their partner will mollify any hurt that either of them may cause. On the negative side, Librans can be frivolous and shallow.

But, on the positive side, Librans seldom get angry, but when circumstances change, they can burst out in a sudden rage. You love pleasure, and may be extravagant. However, men born under this sign may become reckless gamblers, and the women may have the tendency to be extravagant, jealous, or careless. They may squander their wealth and even their talents. Both male and female can be gossipers, if they are not careful. You can be energetic, but you do not like dirty work. Librans are very ambitious and would make good diplomats, but they may not make good politicians, because they are very moderate in their opinions. They tend to see other people's point of view, due to their fairness.

Sun in Libra:

Symbolic to the scale, when the Sun is in Libra: you will crave comfort, because you want no confrontation, pressure, or arguments. You desire peace to be happy, especially in friendships. You are a diplomatic individual, and you can help to quiet the storm in others. Librans worst fault is that they can be indecisive, but nevertheless: they do not want to hurt anyone. You do not like loneliness, so you will have many friends. You are a good listener, and you can be very romantic and charming when you desire to be so. You have the ability to achieve balance between opposing sides. Librans make good business partners, and they work hard to gain business partnerships. Generosity is one of your strong suits, but you have to be careful not to try to trade this for love and affection. You love to earn money, because you love luxurious things. You are very selective with whom you share personal information with, because Librans are very sensitive.

Work is most definitely not the most important thing to Librans, because family is their top priority. Isolation would not agree with you, since you love to travel and explore. You are an adventurer, and you love peace and harmony. "It is also of aesthetic development with strong love of beauty and harmony." (Hand, 1981 p. 225) They do not like fussy people, or people who are slave drivers. Anything in fashion, beauty and cosmetics would gain your attention. You have a legal mind, and law is a good career for you. You are quite the executive, and would make a good business man/woman, or CEO. Librans are very acute and sensitive, which would make a good editor, accountant, teacher, and musician. You have to meditate to bring balance to your life and and peace to your surroundings. You tend to think with your head and not your heart, and that can land you in trouble. Librans "radiate sociable graceful, intellectual vitality and refined sensitivity." (Arroyo, 1989 p. 54)

Moon in Libra:

When the Moon is in Libra, you do not like to be alone, because you thrive for partnerships. Many Librans will marry at a young age, or choose to move in with someone. You are sympathetic, but you love to debate. This brings out your analytical genius, and you love to rapport with individuals on the same intellectual level. You want someone with you all the time. "Feels secure when involved in close relationships; uncomfortable being alone for too long." (Arroyo, 1989 p.59) One of your beliefs is that there is strength in numbers, and that it takes more than one person to get the job done. Because of your charm, you flirt a lot. Librans can be gentle and well refined in their mannerism. You can be indecisive and inconsistent, at times. But, you love to have the last word in every argument, because this is important to you. You will accomplish your goals, especially when you have the help of others. As a Libran, you will make an excellent planner, but delegating to others is something that you will prefer to do.

Paying attention to details, problem solving, and strategizing is something that you are good at. Librans may have mood swings that changes from moment to moment, yet you may appear to be cheerful. However, it is hard to hide your feelings, but you can change your personality to fit the people who you are spending time with. In order to balance things, you would weigh every decision over and over, in order to make the right decision. You love your family and home, and are affectionate and encouraging, always offering support to those you love.

34

With the Moon in Libra, you may tend to be forgetful, and do not cope well with violence and aggression.

Scorpio:

The sign that represents independence is Scorpio. In essence, they are able to accomplish most anything that they put their minds to, and of course, they would not give up. You are insociable and would prefer to be on your own, because you like to be in control. You love change, and tend to be on the mystical side. "This is not the mysticism, ascetic, and self-denying. It is a mysticism that sees the power of transformation at work in ordinary reality." (Hand, 1981 p. 228) Scorpio loves nature and can get in touch with the universe in a physical and spiritual sense. Everything that you do and experience comes from deep within. You love to get in touch with your emotional side. You prefer to love and loss than not to love at all.

When Scorpio is in a relationship, it can be complicated, because they love to go to the extreme. In many cases, they can be moody, for no reason. You are possessive and jealous, but you can be loyal. Because of your excellent memory, you do not let things go. You can hold on to a grudge against someone for a very long time, and you rarely forgive and forget. But, on the other hand, you will remember kind gestures forever, and would most definitely repay it. This will gain trust and respect, from others.

The Sun in Scorpio:

You are intelligent, and both male and female have a deep well of strength, and once it is tapped into, can make you a powerful ally. There is a burst of energy, which is why you are so creative. "Creative energy penetrates surface experience through intense emotional power and intuition." (Arroyo, 1981 p. 54) You do not take anything lightly. You love to express yourself. You are a workaholic, but you tend to produce what you set your mind to produce. Scorpio is a master at using other people's money, in order to build their own fortune. You are very generous to charities and any other worthy cause. You attack a problematic situation in an intriguing, dynamic, and majestic way. However, you struggle between the soul and personality, because your sign is the sign of death.

Scorpio can be their own worst enemy, or their best friend. This is the mystery that lies deep within them; one that make them misunderstood by many. You are creative, but you have a deadly tongue, which in turn, would get you in trouble. It is easy to overcome any obstacles in your path, because you are courageous. You are skillful at hiding your emotions; you can be called a master at doing this. Compassion, humility, purity and service will help you to reach your goals. Because of your mystical side, you love metaphysics. Scorpio love rituals and you will feel a sense of belonging to any religion that does it. You are most likely to have a deep connection with the ethereal world; the spirit world. You are a survivor, and you will help people to transcend themselves. It is difficult to forget an encounter with a Scorpio.

Moon in Scorpio:

The Moon is in fall, when it is in Scorpio. You do a lot of internal dialogue, and you tend to experience emotions deeply. However, when your temper is provoked, you can become explosive. You are conscious of your emotions, because you feel vulnerable and will do your best to keep your feelings to yourself. "Self-image affected by, turbulent emotions. Fear of vulnerability and losing control can lead to emotional regression." (Arroyo, 1989 p. 60) Scorpio is very intense, but does not show their true feelings on their faces. You love completely, totally, and fiercely, but if you despise someone, they would not exist for you.

It is not a good idea to hurt a Scorpio, and if good is not made immediately, Scorpio would have your head. You normally have good hunches, and know how to read between the lines. You know how to listen to a conversation, and pick up on things that others usually do not. You attract drama. When you feel troubled, you will seek out your sanctuary, so that you can find inner peace. Medication would work in a positive manner for Scorpio. You are outspoken and blunt, which accounts for much of his integrity. As a nurturer, you are both protective and possessive. A mother with the Moon in Scorpio can be smothering, and have a challenge in letting go.

Sagittarius:

When it comes to having a positive outlook on life, Sagittarius is the sign that demonstrates this talent. They have a lot of energy, versatility, and they are adventurous. You will love to travel and explore,

36

because your mind is always open to new perceptions and thoughts. Even though your hopes are dashed, you will continue to remain ambitious and optimistic. Not every disappointment would affect you. Because of your passion for justice, you are generous, trustworthy, honest, and honorable. You strive for independence. Once you believe in something, for example, a religious body, you will speak very highly about it. You have to be careful that you do not worship the beliefs of God and not God himself. You have a strong and steady ground, and are unmovable once you set your mind to something. They have philosophical minds, which is equipped with foresight and sound judgment. You are a good conversationalist.

Sagittarians are initiators, especially when it comes to new projects. You have a deep urge to gain an understanding about concepts that are new to you. You are quick on your feet and are a fast thinker, and you are intuitive, but you are a lot better at adapting rather than inventing. It is easy for you to work with colleagues, and you will work well on a team. You are an organizer and is strong willed, which help you to complete projects, successfully. In love, you are straightforward. You love to make your feelings known. When a Sagittarian is saddened, he or she may become bitter his or her whole life or the individual may take revenge on the opposite sex. In a successful marriage, you are faithful to your partner, and you are indulgent parents.

Freedom is important to you, because you do not like to feel pinned down. In friendships, you seldom betray your friends, because you are a loyal friend. Both male and female can be impulsively angry, and would be outspoken when this happens. In most part, you are big on forgiving any offense that someone has done to you. You are a teacher and would make a great philosopher.

"It values personal freedom and self-expression as highly as any other fire sign, and therefore it may have trouble adjusting to the restriction on the larger social order. It prays rule in which to move and freedom with which to express itself." (Hand, 1981, p. 231) Sagittarians would make excellent lawyers, social administrators, politicians, do public service, and public relations, and advertising. You tend to become restless easily, so you would need to move about playing sports, and doing outdoor activities. You would also make a good coach for sports. You are demanding, especially on the job, and you want to be recognized for the work   that you do. You tend to be boastful and extravagant in your private life, and your recklessness can jeopardize your stability. Since Sagittarians governs the hips and sacral region, they may suffer from ailments in those areas. You may also have poor skin, nails, and hair.

The Sun in Sagittarius:

Sun in Sagittarius represents challenge, inquiry, and fascination in an individual. You possess the ability and desire freedom and a variety of things that you are interested in. You will always pursue your interests. You have a compulsion to set goals, but you may not always complete them. Because you are always looking towards the future, it is important that you learn how to control your enthusiasm and optimism, so that you would not lose your focus. Sagittarius need to be recognized, and you may be insensitive to others, because of it. " Needs to be reorganized for moral, upright nature; sometimes high standards can lead to intolerance and insensitivity to others." (Arroyo, 1980 p. 55)

Your biggest strength is meeting challenges. It is imperative to you that you have the space to grow. You are a natural risk taker, and you move too quickly to get caught. Sagittarians areas visionaries, and can be judged, at times, for being too independent. You are idealistic, and you value the ability to liberate yourself from any lower nature, so that you can find your higher self. You are an extrovert, and you are friendly and outgoing. In other words, you are the life of the party. You will spend your money on books, study, and travel, instead of material possessions. You do not like to be constrained and want to work in a job place that offers total freedom, especially when it comes to calling the shots.

Moon in Sagittarius:

You are happy and go lucky, even free-spirited, as long as you are not cooped up. Being physically active is a dream, because you love to socialize. You do not like open space. You are very competitive and you love fresh air. Naturally, you are an athlete. Sagittarians "feels comfortable when exploring, traveling, being outdoors, Loves a sense of freedom."(Arroyo, 1989 p. 60) Usually, you hate routine, and feel the need to escape, if this happens. You are very optimistic and you always believe that everything will work out for the best. There is a quality in you to succeed where others will fail, because you are a risk taker. You tend to be too candid, and should learn how to be tactful.

You are naturally attracted to power and status, and you love to leave an impression on other people who come in contact with. Indeed, you are creative and talented and you can go into the field of arts design. You can have success in sales and educational jobs, because they require you to communicate. You can appear to be two different people, since you have dual personalities. You love to learn, and you will be restless, if you are not intellectually stimulated. As a result, you are adventurous and spontaneous. This is why you would make a great teacher. Of course, you are always enthusiastic about sharing your passions and you are good at explaining what makes the subject so fascinating.

Capricorn:

Interesting enough, the sign that represents hard work is the tenth sign of the zodiac, Capricorn. It is likened to the oldest and most valuable tree in the forest. You will be happy just to put in a full day at the office, because you are ambitious and determined. Life is merely a project for you and you would normally adapt to this in a businesslike approach. Capricorns are very practical, and they normally take things one step at the time. You can be realistic, and you love to do things hands on. You are very dedicated to your goals, of which you can be very stubborn. You love victory, which will definitely keep you going. This motivates you to climb high. You love to be outdoors in the clean fresh air. It is important to you that you go to the top in your chosen field, so that you can reap the benefits.

Fame, prestige, and money are the result of your ambitions. Capricorns tend to walk on some people to get to the top, because they think that it is part of being leader. "The sign would rather control others. Capricorn desires to take the rules it has been taught about the external world and use them as well as possible to build a monument to its own existence. It wants to be able to say to the world "I did it, I built that." (Hand, 1980 p. 233) Ultimately, you are well organized and efficient, and you won't make a lot of waves. You are careful with details, and pay close attention to them. Too often, you play it safe, which is why you are not a risk taker. Patience is definitely a virtue and you are a perfect example of this.

Capricorns expect everyone to be ambitious as they are, and can be unforgiving to others if they do not share this quality. You have to remember that you would need allies along the way, and you should treat others with the respect that they deserve. You have to work hard for what you want, because nothing is handed to you on a silver platter. Capricorns are well disciplined and responsible to get where they need to go. You love truth which is your only reality. "Capricorn is concerned with an objective idea truth that is at the same time experience able. Thus Capricorn arrives at an idea of truth that it grants absolute reality. (Hand, 1980 p. 233) However, you have the tendency to be mature and you have good common sense, which in turn would help your endeavors. You are down to earth, and you would not go chasing any dreams that appear unrealistic. On the other hand, you are very polite and friendly, which is why it is easy for you to make friends.

The Sun in Capricorn:

You have the ambition to be the most successful person in the zodiac, because of discipline. But in some cases, you may lack self-confidence. This can make you use people for your own purposes. You will excel in any business, especially in medicine, engineering, or accounting, editing, politics, building, architecture, and computers. Being pessimistic is one of your worst qualities. "Follow off creative expression can be frozen by pessimism, a cynical attitude, or too much concern with respectability and appearances."(Arroyo, 1980 p. 55) When you are at your best, you are a true leader and you are full of integrity and seriousness. However, your strongest desire is to succeed. You hold additional values close to your heart, and of course, you normally work slowly to achieving in your goals.

These values are based upon the way in which you run your home and the kind of parent you are. In order for someone to gain your respect or get rewarded by you, such individual has to earn it. You can be materialistic and you would say "yes" to the things that money has to offer. It is difficult for you to show your true feelings to anyone, even in an intimate relationship. You may appear to be cold by many, because they do not understand your warm feeling. You want to rule the domain that you possess, whether it is the home or business. You handle money well, but you would spend it on things that you like. You are old fashioned, but you can build an Empire, if you so desire.

Moon in Capricorn:

Whenever the moon is in Capricorn, it translates a sense of responsibility and responsiveness. But, the individual can be cold to human sentiments, and this may diminish any capacity for feeling. "Needs to manipulate the world and others in order to feel secure, comfortable, and to achieve one's goals; can set aside personal concerns to fulfill duties". (Arroyo, 1989 p. 60) Because of your ambitious nature, you can be married to your work; therefore, you do not have a problem submitting to authority. Early in life, you normally learn how to structure a plan of action to succeed, which is a part of your personality. You may encounter problems with either one of your parents, in your childhood.

However, your outward demeanor may be poised and charming, but on the inside, there may be fears, shyness, and you tackle challenges, head on. This can lead to remarkable accomplishments. When someone is not competent, he/she may become frustrated or depressed, which will only result in resentfulness, on the person's part. This stems from a hidden pride, which may impart a desire to gain status, and be noticed by others. You are most likely to succeed in public affairs or any enterprise of any kind. It is important that you examine your inner feelings to decide that you want what you say you want.

Aquarius:

Aquarians are perfect representatives for the Aquarian Age. You tend to have a social conscience that is needed to carry you into a new millennium. You are naturally a humanitarian, and you are the philanthropist, because you have a deep and strong desire to make the world a better place. You are the one to organize the team in a way that they will work and get along with a better understanding. Aquarians normally focus their energy on social institution to help them work better with others. Indeed, you are a perfect visionary, and you progressively spend time thinking on how things can work better for everyone involved. And, of course, you are quick to engage others in this process.

"Aquarius is the first sign of the individual as a cooperative unit of the group. It is a sign in, theoretically at least the individual ego and its needs are subordinated to those of the larger social unit of which the individual is a part. It is true that Aquarians is at its best as part of some kind of social grouping." (Hand, 1981, 236)

You are a gift to the world, and what you have to offer is priceless. Aquarians have a great mind; you are even considered to be a genius. You can be inventive and original, and you will share your ideas as a gift to those who would listen, and you are happier when the world agrees with you. When people disagree with you, they will find out that you can be a bit impatient. When it comes to giving, Aquarians would do this on their own term, and in their comfort level. Freedom is definitely something that you seek, which is why you love to travel. It is important that you explore your individualistic side, so that you can find the sympathetic and compassionate part of who you are. Most importantly, you love it when things go your way, but your heart is always in the right place. Your friends and acquaintances means a lot to you, and you hold them in a special place in your heart.

Aquarians normally think that they are right. You are all about creativity and technology, and you love the latest gadgets for the computer. You have a logical mind, and when you put it to work, you will accomplish much. Of course, you know how to entertain complex and scientific ideas to bring betterment to the organization that you are a part of. One of your qualities is: you are artistic and inventive, which will help you to make a difference. Family and friends would surround you, when you are in the mood to relax. Swimming is something that you would enjoy, including tennis, but since your sign rules the lower leg, you have to be careful not to injure it. Jealousy is not one of your strong suits. You love water colors, because they keep you calm.

The Sun in Aquarius:

The individual with the Sun in Aquarius will get emotionally involved in work, rather than with people. It is difficult for you to establish and maintain close intimate relationships, because of your independence. You have freedom of spirit, and you have a difficult time letting others into your life. But, you are a natural humanitarian. You are both honest and loyal. Because of your intellectual mind, you love to ponder big things. You are stubborn and this may cause detachment from others. Evidently, you do not like others to invade your space. Communicating on a grand scale is of the uttermost importance to you. "Urge to be and to create is colored by freedom, eccentricity, and experimentation. Expression of individuality can be deterred by self-effacement, over-concentration on deity, or aimless rebellion." (Arroyo, 1989 p. 55)

In the fields of technology and psychology, you work well. You are very intuitive, and you may follow your own path. You have an eccentric quest for knowledge and would share it with the world. This helps to bring out the genius in you, because you think in unique and remarkable ways. You are rebellious, yet you have a strong passion for causes. Your compassion comes from the intellectual part of you and not from your heart, but you have a broad spectrum of interests. You have the tendency to be critical and demanding. You will hold on to your ideas, and would not lose hope, which brings out the stubborn streak in you. You are imaginative and would make good story tellers. It is easy for you to get along with almost everyone.

Moon in Aquarius:

Intellectual, intuitive, and intense are some of the attributions to someone with an Aquarius Moon. You will have a deep concern for other people's troubles. An understanding and sympathetic nature, along with observational skills are part of your good powers. You cannot help it, but to be driven to uniting man and woman in equality, which is a part of your humanitarian side. Your love for freedom is connected to your wider political sense, which applies to you personally, as well. It is also important that you express yourself, so that your feelings can be made known. You are an individual and you want to keep your independence. "Responds individualistically, based on sense of self as unique, altruistic, and socially conscious."(Arroyo, 1980 p. 61)

In an intimate relationship, you demand a great deal of freedom from your partner. This is the due to the fact that you need time to settle down in the relationship. Some individuals may not take marriage vows seriously, and would rather to settle down, instead of getting married. Unusual and extraordinary things will attract you, and you grasp ideas easily. You are a dreamer, and you, at times, can get lost in daydreaming, if you are not careful. There is also a playful childlike quality about you, which comes with a great sense of humor. Parents give their children personal freedom, and may find it difficult to impose limits on their behavior. It is almost, as though you expect them to be rebellious. Furthermore, you will encourage them to express their ideas, no matter how strange they may sound.

43

Pisces:

The completion of this cycle gives an individual the final stage of eviction. This brings together many characteristics from the other signs. Pisces are very happy to keeping these qualities under wraps. They focused on their inner journey, spiritually and selfless ways. They are truly humanitarians. In Pisces, the subordination is not a social group but toward the universe itself, and that which repels it.

"Pisces symbolizes the surrender of the soul to God. Whatever one may feel about a God, there is something that makes the universal (the "one turning" in Latin)" (Hand, 1981, p. 239). Metaphysics, mystical, and secret orders will attract you on a deeper level: because your intuitiveness is highly evolved. It is; however, easy for you to go with the flow, without causing any contradictions. This is a true statement because Pisces is unsolidified and easy-going. The two fishes represents they yin and yang sensibility, and at times, the duality may impress upon you giving you a challenge to make up your mind, which turn to make next.

Pisces symbolizes the end of one phase, and the beginning of another. "Another aspect of Pisces must be understood: it is both and end and a beginning. As such, it stands for the stage just prior to the birth of the new self. Pisces at the end of a cycle indicated surrender of the mature self is a prelude to rebirth."(Hand, 1980 p. 239) It is easy for you to recognize between what is reality and what is not, by using your introspective nature. You can take a personal and inner voyage into the conscious and subconscious easily, which is part of your intuitive nature. It is not easy to pin you down, and you would not stay away for long, since one of your primary goals is to help others. You give freely of yourself, without expecting anything in return.

Of course, this is because you are compassionate and charitable in nature. Your self-sacrifice keeps you going. On the flipside, others may take advantage of you, so it is vital that you use your intuitions. Pisces can get caught up in their dreams in view of things and how they should be. In other words, you are melancholy. When this happens, you should take time for yourself, so that you can recharge and be grounded once again. You feel deeply, and often times, are misunderstood. You are very sensitive, and you would treat your lover with love and caring. You are

44

quite the romantic. You are talented in music and painting, and you love water sports and swimming.

The sun in Pisces:

The individual can have conflict with the self; because there is always a pulling in the opposite direction. In this case, it is a representation of the personality tied to the soul with one swallowing the other. Service is your motto. You sacrifice the self on behalf of others. This individual "needs to be recognized for compassionate, giving nature."(Arroyo, 1980 p. 56). On a larger scale, it may be difficult for you to face reality, and people may feel deceived by you. It is imperative that you remain focus, so that you can channel your creative imaginations in the right directions, because you are considered to be the poet of the zodiac. Organization is not one of your best skills, but you can be creative working in the background. Because you are aware of the suffering of others, you would make an excellent counselor. Some of the careers that are best suited for you are: religious, musicians, doctors, designer, and administrators.

Variety is something that you crave. On a deeper and spiritual self, you are always preparing to retreat from things that are on the outside of you, so that you will eliminate any conflict, and seek balance. There is a source that you may refer to as the River of life, where you can find the strength to accomplish everything that you set your mind to. You would explore your world through your emotions, so that you can concentrate on your solitude and the life force within. As a woman, you can be mysterious, complex and compassionate. She has a quiet enough strength that doesn't allow her to be limited in her expressions, yet she craves companionship, and solitude. As a man, you displayed the quiet strength. You are self-contained and are a good listener, and you will give your individual attention. You can be played for a sucker. Indeed, you are a true romantic. You will wine and dine your mate. Once you are smitten, your emotions will run deep and eternal.

Moon in Pisces:

Those who are born with their Moon in this sign have strong intuitive feelings. It is easy for them to walk a mile in someone else's shoes. You are full of love and feelings, and you can lose yourself in other problems. You are naturally romantic and would never forget about a gift on Valentine's Day or someone's birthday. "Nurture others through healing compassionate and sympathy; feel secure when serving humanity or a spiritual ideal."(Arroyo, 1981 p.61). You possess a wonderful sense of humor and you are easily aroused. You are misunderstood by many, but you are deeper than they think. Becoming overwhelmed with reality would help you to drift. You are sweet and soft hearted, because you genuinely care about others.

You look for yourself in everyone, which makes it easy for you to help them. It is also imperative that you do not absorb what others are feeling. There is a shyness about you, but you would make a great artist, writer or musician. You must take care of yourself, so that you would not get walked upon. Taking a break from people and circumstances would help to prevent this from happening. You are very sensitive and can get hurt by rejection or insults. Indeed, you are a natural philosopher. You are a loyal friend, and you are able to see beauty in all forms. You do your best to avoid the boring things in life, because you love excitement. It is also important to nurture and cultivate your sensitivity. It is necessary that you have a meaning in life, in case of any un-appreciation from others, you would not feel discouraged.

The Houses:

The area of your mind, the astrological houses, which begins from the tip of the ascendant. They rise from the eastern horizon at the time of birth. The houses are just like the zodiac, because the sky is divided into twelve sections. There is imperative information about the spheres, and some of them receive more weight than others, which differs from person to person. The geographical location is determined at the exact time of birth. The houses are aligned with the Earth's rotation, which makes a complete revolution in twenty-four hours. Furthermore, the houses indicate where the altitudes, activities, and the particular energy, which are represented by the planet is likely to manifest.

The Houses:
Ascendant:

In order to know where the first house lies, it is important to know the exact time of birth. The first house is referred to as the Ascendant, which gives you a deeper understanding of the individual. "Making the cusp of the 1st house, the Ascendant shows the exact degree of the zodiac

46

sign which arises over the eastern horizon at the time of birth." (Greene, 1985 p. 37). This is the beginning of a cycle, which represents the immediate self, and the projective persona. Also, it says a lot about your health. The sign of the cusp will reveal how we express ourselves, and indicating the process of what we are becoming. Coincidentally, it reflects the light from the darkness.

Furthermore, the Ascendant helps us to sort things out through the selection that we meet. Most importantly, this house helps us to meet the world and is also known as the Rising Sun. It gives a description of our appearance and image, also the planets in this house are used to communicate something about the individuality of the person. This is where the heaven and earth is joined in the ecliptic east. "Because the Ascendant corresponds with the initial 'flash' or 'hit' of our individual existence, it also impresses itself deeply into the psyche as that which life is or about." (Greene, 1985 p. 38). However, the Ascendant is the most important feature in the astrological chart. The first, second, and third houses are in deferred quadrant. It allows you to find the development of the self and your environment.

Additionally, an individual may react differently, depending on which sign the Ascendant is in. As an example, if the Ascendant is in Sagittarius, you may identify with a world of excitement and new possibilities, and of course, you would want to explore the world, so that you can grow. An Ascendant in Gemini will give you the opportunity to seek and obtain knowledge, so that you can gain a deeper level of understanding. One of your most important quest is to figure out what life is all about, and tackle and conquer it head on. The Ascendant signifies the combination of the self, self-identity and self-concern; helps you to focus on the self.

The second house:
Within the first quadrant lies the second house. "The traditional labeling of the second house makes it sounds as if it covers only that which is concrete and tangible and of interest to the inspector." (Greene, 1985 p. 43). Indeed, the second house deals with your possessions and how you deal with money. It is important for you to develop your self-worth, because this is important to you as an individual. You may be ego driven, as well. You will definitely become conscious of your appearance and your buddy, and how it explains who you are and how others perceive

47

you as an entity. Stability is also connected to the second house, and you would want balance in everything that you do.

"As time goes by we will develop a sense of other things we possess besides the body-a good mind, a clever tongue, a sympathetic nature, a practical ability, and artistic flair, etc." (Sasportas, & Greene, 1985 p. 44). You, however, would have a strong need to be safe, and secure. If the second house is in Gemini, you would have a need to possess knowledge because you will understand how to use this knowledge which will keep you safe. Your innate ability is part of the second house. Your goals and how you would accomplish them is also part of your self-worth, as this is part of your desires. Sacrificing and letting go will give you the initial sense of gain.

In this house, you are more aware of the self as being a part of the universe, which becomes a part of your total being. It indicates someone's attitude towards money and possessions, and anything that you can be attached to. The way in which the individual acts, based on his or her experiences is a symbol of the second house.

The third house:
The house of the communication is the third house. It identifies and governs all forms of a communication, and how one expresses the self. Relationships with siblings, relatives, and neighbors will reveal how you interact with them. Also, the way in, which you handle your documents and your writing demonstrates an important aspect of this house. "The key phrase in as "I think". This procedure implies the faculty of conscious thought, the domain of the third house. We are constantly creating ourselves in the image of whatever our thoughts are focused upon." (Sakoian & Archer, 1973 p. 85).

However, it reflects and represents your understanding and how you interact with the community. The third house initially rules the rational thought and conscious state of mind. How your memory works, especially through your early childhood education, and how you speak. It is imperative for you to be mindful of how you possess your thought pattern, because it creates your destiny. With Mercury sitting in the house, it is imperative that you choose your thoughts process wisely, because the actions that you take will be a direct result of your reality, which can lead to positive and negative actions. Furthermore, "Gemini, is ruled by

48

Mercury, this house is concerned with assimilation, processing, and circulation of information. It is the house of the practical mind, and since necessarily imply the communication of ideas, this is the first of the air houses that concerns brothers and sisters near neighbors and people in general." (Sakoian, & Archer, 1973 p. 86)

However, your traveling is also a part of the third house. Who and what influence us and whether or not your mind is mature enough to handle everything that is going on in and around you, and how the mind continues to develop and unfolds.

The fourth house:

Your emotional, subconscious self-image, and foundation is based on the fourth house. The way in which you feel about yourself is actually a condition of your individual experience with your parents, or anyone with whom you have a relationship with, while growing up. "The fourth house rules of the accumulated environmental conditions we have created for ourselves, primarily the domestic scene. As we appropriate resources, will build up a base of operations, which functions also as a source of security." (Sakoian & Archer, 1973 p.87)

Furthermore, this applies to how you express yourself in the home, and how you would eventually take care of your household items. Your immediate environment will be a clear indication of what you are harboring in your mind or how disciplined the mind is. This is a combination of your psychological environment, which is a part of the unconscious state of being. Everything that is suppressed inward will automatically be expressed outward. You will yearn for emotional support, because you want to belong to something or someone. The fourth house is ruled by the Moon, and it governs women, so it can be inferred that the mother is found in the fourth house.

The fifth house:

Your children are in the fifth house, and the way in which you relate to them. How you amuse and entertain yourself, along with self-expression is a natural part of the fifth house. This is part of your energy. How many children you have, or whether or not you choose to have any will be defined in this house. "The Fifth House is the house of creative expression. It represents the next stage of an individual's development. The Fifth House rules the children of the mind and body and has to do

49

with all creative arts, especially the performing arts." (Sakoian, & Archer, 1973 p. 88). In this house, you will learn how to organize your thoughts in order to build a firm foundation. How you conduct your investments is an integral part of this house.

Also, the way in, which you bring up your children and how you choose to educate them are revealed in this house. You will be full of joy and will want to express it in creative ways. It is important for you to express yourself. "Another keynote of the 5th is the generativity_which simply defined means 'the ability to produce'. The 5th house is the area of the chart attributed to creative expression, most obviously with artistic endeavor, although the creativity of the 5th needn't be just painted a picture." (Sasportas, & Greene, 1985 p. 61). People may create spontaneously in a joyfully manner. Recreation is another form of creative expression, and you will enjoy the joy of winning. Participate in and what you do is an opportunity that is very important to you.

The sixth house:

"The sixth house is all about sticking to our plan and blossoming into precisely what we were meant to be. Doing this feels right and good. But the consequences for not representing the truths of our own nature of stress, frustration and dis-ease." (Sasportas, & Greene 1985 p. 66). In this house, people are very health conscious, but illness may be found in this house. It is imperative that you take proactive measures, such like diet and exercise. Because people would take hygiene seriously, some of them need to be careful not to become too obsessive about it. Being able to define what is going on both on the outside and inside of you can be important, since you would want to distinguish between the two.

In fact, the sixth house represents service, and how well you serve others. "We are 'designed' in a certain way to serve a purpose or function specified in our own individual on make-up on nature. We serve best by being who we are." (Sasportas, & Greene, 1987 p. 67). Finding your true purpose in life helps you to govern yourself at a deeper level, which will bring satisfaction. The way in which you get along with your coworkers is a placement of the sixth house. The way in, which you lead or dispense your authority is an important aspect to this house. The way you form bonds with others are also shown in the sixth house, and if you lose your animal especially to death, you may go through a psychological strain.

The seventh house:

"When we arrived at the Descendent, the westernmost point in the chart, we turn a sharp corner and find ourselves heading back again to the point where it all started." (Sasportas, & Greene, 1985 p.71). The Descendent represents the point in time when things change for you. Changes are made and you will embrace them, while moving forward. This is the beginning of the Seventh House, which is opposite the Ascendant. You will become more aware of the people with whom you develop strong ties with, and in most parts, you may want to please them. This is the house of "the non-self". It is important that your commitment is mutual, as that and understanding can be a place of common ground. The seventh house is the house of marriage and partnerships, which of course has to do with verbal commitments, whether it is against rivals or one-to-one relationships.

"In the 7th house, two people come together for a purpose person-to enhance the quality of their lives by joining with one another, to produce a family and gain a greater security and stability." (Sasportas, & Greene 1985 p. 72).Because the Descendant is the cusp of the Seventh House, the things that are hidden in you will be revealed, and your qualities, whether you realize they are there or not. There are some things that you may not be aware of and they normally will show up in others that you come into contact with. In the seventh house; however, you are able to find the potential that is locked up on the inside of you. One of the most important things about the seventh house is to bring balance, so that you can identify with the individual self.

The eight house:

Transformation and change is the essence of the eight house. The things that you want to die and resurrect are attached to this house. You would let go of the old things to embrace the new things. "Signs and planets in the eight house suggests how we fare financially in marriage, inheritance or business partnerships." (Sasportas, & Greene, 1985 p. 76). You will find it easy to handle other people's finances, and you will make an excellent stockbroker and accountant. The way in which you negotiate and relate too and with others is another attribution of the eight house. Open communication will bring peace to your relationship.

Coming together with another individual would form a bond; a union of two becoming one. In the eight house, your sexual pleasure is revealed. Your relationships will help to bring the change that you would desire. Whatever you have suppressed, will come to the surface, and they shall be visible. There are things that you have not dealt with, whether it was ill feelings between you and loved ones. If for some reason, you have had fears about relationships, they will come to the forefront if you are feeling insecure in the one you are in, at the moment. "The fear that our partner doesn't love us anymore or is possibly betraying us will trigger or reawaken the primal fears or the loss of the original love-object." (Sasportas, & Greene, 1985 p. 78). This is due to the experiences that you may have experienced during childhood.

In order for transformation to take place, you must first, go within yourself and change the things that have caused it, in the first place. You will do this by recognizing all the good that lies on the inside of you. Your childhood experiences and how you viewed your father is something that you have to deal with, because a woman would think and attract the same man. However, as you become more mature, you can clean out those fears that are deeply rooted within the subconscious mind. "All levels of shared experience described by the 8th house. In addition to the realm of joint finance and the merging of two individuals into one, this house has a broader slant. (Sasportas, & Greene, 1985 p.80)

The ninth house:

All off someone's mental functions, and how the individual deals with the day to day routine is a true symbol of the ninth house. Your ideas and how you perceive things is a true example of how your conscious mind is expanding. You do not just want to know things, but you want to know and understand the meaning of what you have learned. The ninth house also deals with long-distance travel, especially to foreign countries. People who are strongly influenced by the ninth house will be motivated in religion, theology, philosophy, higher learning, books, publishing, expanding, and prophecy.

"The 9th house is that area of the chart most directly concerned with philosophy and religion. It is here that we seek truth, endeavoring to fathom the underlying patterns and basic laws which governs life." (Sasportas, & Greene, 1985 p.82). It is important to understand how to direct your life in the direction that you desire for it to go. When your life has meaning, then you will have something to live for and look forward to. People usually discover God's plan for their lives and how they can make a deeper spiritual connection. You love to socialize and mix with people, and you are a cultural person; you love to learn about other cultures and how people live. "Placements in the 9th designate the archetypal principles we encounter on our travels, and may even reveal something about the nature of the culture or cultures to which we are drawn." (Sasportas, & Greene, 1985 p.85).

The tenth house:

Evidently, the cusp off the tenth house is formed by the Midheaven (MC), which is the highest point of the chart. Therefore, everything stands out in this house. As an individual, you become more visible and it is easier for others to have access to you. How you operate in society is more important than your own personal scope of things. Your responsibilities in the public place is of importance, because you are concerned about how you conduct your professional life. People who are influenced by the Midheaven will make good politicians. "The Midheaven is the most elevated point in the chart, and symbolically speaking, placements here 'stand out' above all others. (Sasportas, & Greene, 1985 p. 87).

However, the tenth house reveals the ambition in someone. The individual's career path will be described. You yearned for space and freedom, and you want to be recognized, which is more about prestige. "The tenth House, the planets place therein, and aspects made to the planets, along with the ruler of the house and the signed placed on it, government the ability. The Tenth House shows how ambitious one is and how ambition is manifested." (Sakoian, & Greene, 1973 p. 92)

The eleventh house:

In terms of groups of and how they express their creativity, not as an individual, but as a body, the eleventh House reflects this. Your ability to think and create will be disclosed. Your traits and goals normally come true. Your role in the community, and your social acquaintances and how you relate to them are all a part of your creative flow. You will give to charities because you are a natural humanitarian. When you are a part of a group, you only focus on the purpose of the group, and how it can achieve success. People take friendship seriously, and will protect their friends. You would not operate in isolation, because you know that you cannot do anything by yourself, but being a part of a system would get the job done.

53

"The components of the systems and their attributes are viewed as functions of the total system. The behavior and expression of each variable influences and is influenced by all the others. With the needs of the system as a whole." (Sasportas, & Greene 1985 p. 92) Individuals who are a part of a group, and is influenced by the eleventh house understand how important safety in numbers are. Your main goal is: how to accomplish the greater good, and how comfortable you feel in the group. Expanding your boundaries and borders and are also a significant aspect in this house, which is a quality that you possess.

The twelfth house:

When people have a desire to hide things, it is found in the twelfth house. They would have secrets, and may want to do things in seclusion. You can be a part of mystical groups, and will possess a deep intuition. People who are influenced by the twelfth house would have to be mindful how they consume alcohol. There are signs that you may be prone to depression. This house is the end of the cycle, so it will give you an option for new beginning. There is a deep needed for you to reconnect to loved ones and someone that is dear to you. "One strategy for reconnecting to unity is through sex and love. 'If I am loved, included, then I go beyond my separateness. Another play to regain a lost sense of omnipotence and omnipresence is through wielding power and prestige." (Sasportas, & Greene, 1985 p.99)

Planet in houses:

There is a relationship between the planets and the houses. According to Rudhyar (1992) "On the other hand, the planet in a house indicates that the basic type of experiences to which the house refers can be handled to the best advantage." (p. 176) There is a relationship with the character, which represents the house and how they function. Furthermore, there is a natural rhythm between the house and the planet. The position of the Sun will reveal a specific area of life where you will feel the need to feel special. At this point, you will also feel the need to distinguish yourself. The Sun shows activity, but it is not reactive. If you want to find happiness and direction, the forces of the Sun can reveal this. In fact, you will want to shine, so you will take action, because the Sun cannot be hidden.

The Sun:

The Sun is considered to be one of the most important parts of astrology, and one of the most important astrological planets. The Sun was represented by Apollo (the god of light) in Greek mythology. It is the star in the center of our solar system, and the Earth and other planets revolve, which provides light and heat. The Sun represents the conscious ego; the self-expression personal power. It exemplifies the leadership qualities, spontaneity, life force, health and vitality, pride and authority in an individual. It rules the fun side of life, from holidays and social events and, sports and recreation.

"One of the most important points in the chart, the Sun represents the energy that enables everything else to exist. It is the basic energy of Being. Just as the physical Sun shines and enables all the other bodies to shine by reflecting its light, so the symbolic astrological Sun is the basic energy of which all the other planetary energies are specialized reflections." (Hand, 1981, p. 47)

It symbolizes the Yang and is the ruler planet for Leo. It also represents the life path of the individual and one's vitality. The Sun is central to life and it rules the heart and the spine. It is also considered to be the seat of love. When the Sun is well aspected in someone's chart, it describes the individual as someone who has heart; one who cares for others, whether it is personal or in general. But, when the Sun is poorly aspected, it describes a person who has difficulty accessing love and caring abilities, or who can feel it internally, but does not know how to express it. When the Sun is in detriment, the individual may have difficulty in accessing self-awareness.

The expression of love then becomes less personal and more collective. If the Sun is in fall in Libra, it is in detriment, but the focus becomes narrower to "you and me", because you naturally give meaning to me. However, when the Sun is in detriment in someone's sign, it does not mean that he or she cannot love, but that they would love differently. The Sun also represents what the individual will stand up for, especially the things that the person believes in. In fact, a well aspected Sun will stand up and say "no", if an injustice occurred. But, on the other hand, when the Sun is afflicted, the individual would feel no on the inside, but would lack the ability to say it.

55

People whose Sun is strong would normally stand up for what they believe in; they are very vocal and active about what it right and wrong. On the other hand, weak Sun people keep quiet, and they look the other way. They may care, but they lack the ability to express themselves, and their sense of inner authority literally breaks. It is our self-creativity, because who we are will determine what we make of ourselves, and in turn: our lives. "As yang, the Sun is the archetypal of will, power, and desire, but not necessarily sexual desire. It has the meaning of "waiting to." It represents the energy that exerts itself upon and influences whatever may exist." (Hand, 1981, p. 48)

The Sun is not too accepting, because it always seeks to change and develop, which really seeks from self-expression of inner consciousness. It gives an individual the integrity as a being, and represents the individual's will to exist. It actually pawns pressure from the environment that seeks to make the individual something that he or she is not. It is the model of a hero; one who brings order where there is chaos through his daunting will. In order to prove his strength, he undertakes severe trials against the power of darkness. This makes him worthy. But, when the Sun sets, there is a challenge with darkness, and in the end he would prove himself and rise at the crack of dawn, triumphantly.

All this can be seen in the personality of someone with a strongly placed Sun. Whenever someone gets the occasion to shine, he or she will, just like the sun; and would have to deal with the battles of inner darkness that is embedded within the subconscious mind. Also, the Sun can be considered the mysteries of the universe, and it symbolizes our spiritual and psychological midpoint. "The symbol of the Sun is that of a circle surrounding a point. The circle represents the infinite and unlimited potential of spirit. The dot represents the point where the infinite manifests into finite form." (Bloch, & George, 2006 p. 54)

It depicts our uniqueness; our ability to identify with who we really are. It is important to be in touch with our Sun, so that we would not lack confidence and faith in ourselves. The Sun describes the basic nature of an individual, and any personality traits that remain constant through the ups and downs in life. It really represents the image that you present to the world, but this comes from the factual innermost part of you. It also signifies the way in, which you are vital and powerful in life, and shows what type of environment lights you up. When it comes to pursuit of a mate, the Sun will show how your ego propels you into new experiences.

Furthermore, the Sun is also used to predict a development in an individual's life, by bringing energy to the event. For some reason, the individual may have a waning in his or her energy, if the Sun is weakened. However, women may have a propensity to experience their solar energies, as that of men. Although the Sun is considered yang (male), some women are the employers, so their role as solar would be that of male. But, there are some men who are not very yang temperament, so they would not be able to manifest the solar symbolism. One of the definitive male function that is connected to the Sun is fatherhood.

The Sun in the houses:

"In each house the Sun indicates that the kind of experiences to which the house refers will tend to call for a spontaneous and at least relatively forceful release of fight that energy." (Rudhyar, 1972 p. 178) You will be full of energy and vitality, when the Sun is in the first house and you will yearn for recognition. You will search for an identity, and can be successful. In the second house, however, the Sun displays the individual's need to produce. You will look for different ways to produce wealth, so that you can manifest money. People with the Sun in the second house has as vitality and can become possessive. You want to identify strongly with the image that you present to others, because you have the ability make an impression on others. Your strong will power to make and to manage money will definitely add to your personality.

When the Sun is in the third house, it is imperative for you to be active. You would need to change your scenery often, because you will feel restless, easily. You are proud of your mental ability, and you can make friends, easily. You are quite adaptable in the environment that you are in. There is a solid need for you to communicate your knowledge and ideas to others, so that they can learn. You are curious and it will lead to new discoveries of the self, others, and new ideas, and you take pride in that. You love to be in the know. It is important to you to be good at what you do. In the fourth house, the Sun shows that you would invest much of your energy into your personal and private life. You are a private person; and you are very productive. Part of your basic strategy in life is to plan for the long run.

You believe in taking care of your emotional interests before you can focus on anything else. "The Sun stresses unifying power of inner experiences of personal integration, and in many cases, suggested a vital contact with one ancestry, home, and tradition. Self-reliance and a deep belief in one's "source" can be characteristic of such a solar system." (Rudhyar, 1972 p. 179) Sun in the fifth house demonstrates that you want to be noticed for your special and unique qualities, also your creativity. You are happiest when you are expressing yourself in a special way, which brings attention to you as a result. You love drama, and you are proud of your fun-loving attitude towards life. You will find creative ways to express yourself because this is the path to your true happiness.

There is an inner restlessness about you, and you crave for an outlet through social, drama, and romantic actions. In your search for freedom and self-expression, pleasure and amusement plays an important role. Creative expression is one of your personal powers, which will, work well with leadership and your love for technology. "The Sun may, yet need not, reveal artistic creativity and radiant spontaneity in self-expression. There can also be a strong urge for the use of power and perhaps leadership, particularly in situations which calls for intense vitality." (Rudhyar, 1972 p. 179) Work that you do, and services that you offer is very important to your sense of identity, when the Sun is in the sixth house. When you are busy with daily activities, and produce work that you are proud of, this make you feel proud of yourself for, your accomplishments.

You would need to find an avenue for expressing yourself. You work best when you create your own schedule. One of the important things to you is to receive positive feedback for services you render. Any motivation to do a good job should come from within yourself and not from others. You will seek perfection for the work that you do. You will be able to overcome, weakness, which can relate to health matters. When the Sun is in the seventh house, you will definitely take pride in your ability to negotiate and create harmony in your relationships. This is very important to you because it is important to for you to have a partner, because you feel incomplete without one.

You can be sensitive to rejection, because you are especially motivated to be well-liked. Your social skills can help you to seek peaceful relations with others. You will do better in life when you undertake tasks with others, rather than doing them by yourself. You will give yourself in great measure to your partner because you love to give. You have good manners and charm, and you will be successful in organizations and associations that you are in. The position of the Sun in the seventh house suggests success in marriage is possible. Do not allow impatience to get the better of you, because the union will come when both of you have been matured. You will eventually choose a strong, capable and authoritative partner; one of whom you will be proud of. Furthermore, you are more than likely to win judgment or any litigation that you find yourself involved in.

Eventually, you will have the urge to go farther in life, because you want to experience more and your desires are powerful and intense, when the Sun is in the eighth house. If you choose your magnetic power that you possess you will find satisfaction in your experiences. Fascination comes from what lies on the inside of you, and beneath the surface, which helps to bring self-empowerment. "The Sun may bless the fruits of any relationships and all that increase and illuminate the feeling of closely union with him on integration into a group process, a social or occult ritual." (Rudhyar, 1972 p. 180) You will feel a deep desire to investigate the mysteries or take an interest in occult or metaphysical studies. By doing this, your knowledge will be increased and you will recognize that there is a demand for constant change.

When the Sun is in the ninth house you would have a deep desire and the need to understand the world around you. You have high morals, as you have your eyes set on the horizon. At times, you can seem to be restless, because you are looking ahead, and because of this: you are proud of your principles and knowledge. You acquire this knowledge because of your curious nature. People with the Sun in the ninth house are tolerant and adventurous, and most importantly, they want to see the best in people and life. You have a hunger for learning, and it extends beyond the classroom. Your ability to learn its enhanced by understanding and learning about people and cultures, and you love to learn other languages. Teaching is something that you will also love to do, which of course will give you the ability to earn more than one degree. Because you love to touch the lives of others; you understand that all men are brothers, and they are only separated by restrictions. You are admired because of this.

You will share your wisdom to overcome prejudice. When you have an urge to work towards your goal, so that you can achieve success and accomplishment, your Sun is in the tenth house. You have a hard time taking orders from another individual, which makes you uncomfortable. You are very ambitious, and you feel the need to be in authority. With this in mind, it is imperative for you to function in a career where you manage rather than being managed. "The Sun in the house can mean outer success, leadership, social power and prestige. It can also mean that the basic energy of one's nature will be called upon more or less constantly to handle difficult, even negative situations." (Rudhyar, 1972 p. 181) Basically, you have a natural ability to lead others, and you can excel in a professional manner, because you put a lot of energy into your work.

Realistically, you will be successful as a politician, or in any leadership position. For men, you will have a father figure influence on others, which will help you to educate yourself. However, people with the Sun in the eleventh house are humanitarians, and their aim is to treat everyone as equals. You strive for your uniqueness and originality, and you avoid any prejudice and biasness. Social status does not mean anything to you, because your identity is linked to something bigger than yourself. You are able to take advantage of opportunities, and you have goals that you know that you can accomplish. People are naturally drawn to you because you are open and tolerant. It is easy for you to be everybody's friend, but you do not consider everyone a friend, but those who you consider to be your friend are your friend for a lifetime. If for some reason, you do not have anything in common with someone, you will separate yourself from that person.

Furthermore, it is easy for you to hold more than one office. Because you know how to adapt easily, it is easy to get the most out of any situation. You will not compromise your morals and you will maintain peace and harmony by finding values that can represent who you are. "The Sun is in the twelfth house tends to throw light on the "unfinished business" of the past. Though cleaning up of Karma may become a central life work, which may mean the cleaning of the subconscious repudiation." (Rudhyar, 1972 p. 181) This is due to the fact that you can be an introspective, and would need space and you will seclude yourself to gain strength. Normally, you will avoid the spotlight, and you will hide yourself behind the role, if you find yourself in the public. When serving

60

others, you tend to shine. You are compassionate, which sets you apart from others.

The Moon in the houses:

The Moon in the houses will disclose how we go about our emotional satisfaction. There are emotional clues that can be found through the position of the moon in the houses. It takes the form of constant changes, whether it is ups or downs in the areas of life. It represents our deepest personal needs, our basic habits, and our unconscious mind. It is also associated with the feminine aspect, which are the inner mother and inner child. It also reveals how we protect and make ourselves feel secure, comfortable and safe. The Moon also gives us animation, and also rules the ebb and flow of the activity and energy. It mediates between the inner and outer world. Also, the Moon impacts the past into our lives through deep feelings. When an individual is creative, intuitive, sentimental, adoptable, introspective, and protective, he or she is acting out the Moon.

The Moon in the first house:

You display your feelings for everyone to see, which make you come across as emotional, nurturing and impatient. Your initial reaction is emotional, especially if the Moon is in close range, within 10° of the Ascendant degree. You would need emotional stimulation and freedom to express yourself, so that you can feel fulfilled, which will make you happy. You experience mood swings and it is changeable, and this is obvious to others. You tend to take things too personally, which of course make you react quickly. You are aware of other people's emotions, because it is important to you. You relate sympathetically and emotionally to others because of your soft exterior.

However, your emotions can overpower your logic and reasoning. You appear to be gentle and impressionable to others. It is hard for you to hide your emotions. You most often waver between the feeling good about yourself and sometimes you are down on yourself. You have inconsistent emotions, but you must make a conscious effort to sustain a positive outlook on life. Your moods can be difficult, and you keep those around you on their toes. They do not know how to pin down your moods, because you are a very moody person.

The Moon in the second house:

"In your desire to have everything that will make you more comfortable, you sometimes take chances that you later regret." (Pelletier, 1978 p. 38) When you are dealing with money, you can be too playful in your spending habits. You can also be very generous towards others. You have a fear of being in debt, and feel the need that your bills should be paid on time, and when they are paid, you feel a sense of security. You do not like being without. But on the other hand, you can be quite the impulsive spender. This happens when you feel emotionally frustrated. You tend to hold onto people too tightly. You love to be admired, which can make you dependent on others.

You must develop your feelings of self-worth, so that you would not depend on others for positive feedback. You hold back before expressing yourself. You are a collector, and will collect antiques and sentimental things. You can most definitely expect some changing circumstance surrounding money, when the Moon is in this house. There is a strong need to feel secure about what you have; and there is an emotional attachment to your idea of financial success. You have a tendency to alternate between impulsive generosity and holding onto money.

The Moon in the third house:

With the Moon in this house, you tend to be communicative, curious, and responsive. You will be able to intimidate others and can pick up on language quite easily. It is quite easy for you to communicate what you feel with excessive emotion. You can find a balance with how you multitask doing daily routines. You tend to change ideas, and opinions change quite often. One of the easiest things for you to do is adapt to other people's ideas and express them as if it is your own. This is due to the fact that you are sensitive to other people's opinions. Because you can be restless or nervous, you would need to change scenery frequently.

When something feels right, you make decisions based on that inner unction. You will change this because you feel uncomfortable. You are most comfortable talking about personal subjects, feelings and sharing confidences, and others shared their feelings with you as well. You are an imaginative individual, and there is a strong need to communicate and to express your ideas. There is a strong need to be heard, and of course, you would like others to appreciate what you have to add, especially in an intellectual manner.

The Moon in the fourth house:

There is a longing for a sense of belonging and you may be restless in search of it. You may change residence quite frequently, and you will feel the need to make changes in the home. This may be a healthy thing for you, if it keeps you emotionally stimulated. Also, you may be emotionally immature, and you may want to grow up. You have a strong attachment to your past, traditions and family. The place where you grew up will be seated in your memory. "The Moon in the fourth house well aspected indicates fortunate home conditions. It also shows many changes in residences which will be fortunate or otherwise according to the other aspects of the moon." (Hand, & Foss Nendil, 1973 p. 222)

It can be quite difficult for you to let go of habits that you have learned, during your childhood. You tend to have a strong tie towards your mother, which may cause you to seek mothering from your spouse. There is a need for you to have a secure home, and having a certain amount of privacy, because this is very important to you. There will be a number of changes that you will make to your residence; you will live in more than one home. And, if this applies to you, stability will come later in life.

The Moon in the fifth house:

Your emotional experience is something that you love to share with loved ones. This can give you a dramatic flair. Your love affair is both intense and magnetic, and you do not take your mate lightly. You will go through changes in your romance. There is a strong attachment to children, whether or not they are your own. You have natural artistic talents. You have a vivid imagination which can make you daydream. Often times, you will find yourself getting in touch with your inner child. However, you may have problems with gambling, frequent love affairs, or impulsive shopping. In fact, you are more attracted to the game than the player.

There is an exciting part of you that would love to take risks, just for the fun of it. You would not make any pretense about your feelings or your personal sympathies towards others. There will be many ups and downs, because the Moon is indecisive in this house, in respect to love and social involvement. But, there is a great need to pursue these things. You are an intuitively romantic and the feeling that you are in love gives you the sentiment that it satisfies your emotional needs.

The Moon in the sixth house:

It is important to you that you lead a healthy life, and that you are organized and on top of things. Also, you work productively and have an emotional need to be useful. However, if there is chaos in any of these, then there will be on emotional unrest. There is also a need for variety on the job, so that you can feel stimulated. This will make you happy. There are some of you that will change jobs often, so that you can find the perfect job fit. You tend to be a very sensitive person, which makes you aware of health annoyances, such as body aches. "Functional difficulties in physical body. If afflicted apt to have stomach difficulties due to distorted emotional attitudes." (Hickey, 1999 p. 150)

You must expect many changes, when it comes to the work that you do, because they are only jobs that you will take, in order for you to survive. These jobs will be a means to an end, so that you can pay the bills. You are the individual that takes serving to heart, and will have a heart to take care of others. You are the type who will want order and structure in your home environment.

The Moon in the seventh house:

You are an individual that is drawn to partnerships, and of course you desire to have a companion for emotional support. You love to be in the company of others, especially if you are taking in a movie or having dinner. Your partner will stimulate feelings in you that you may not be aware of, and you may need this to learn more about yourself. You do not like to be alone, so you tend to jump from relationship to relationship without taking enough time in between them. You are likable and adaptable to other people's needs, but you may be dependent on other people for emotional support.

You will have many friends who care about you, and you will treat them as though they are your kin. For some reason, you tend to be very dependent and somewhat unsure of yourself without a close partner. You are the type that longs for and yearns to experience close and committed relationships, mostly in marriage, business, or with best friends. However, with the Moon in this house, there may be numerous changes in business partnerships. You can instinctively move with the flow with your peer group, because you are rationally inclined to harmony and would avoid conflicts.

The Moon in the eight house:

You are "very sensitive where others are concerned. Can be too vulnerable. Personality must be concerned with helping others." (Hickey, 1992 p. 150) This will give you a strong need for emotional support. You may also feel the need to change your lifestyle. You are fascinated with the hidden things, and how people work. You can be a very mystical person. You change sexual partners frequently, which is a sign of emotional insecurity. Also, you may struggle with jealousy or possessiveness. You can be loyal, deep and intimate to your partner. In many cases, you may not trust others who are trying to get to know you, even though you yearn to be close to others.

When it comes to your feelings, you are true and you tend to want all or nothing. You have a conventional ability to handle other people's money. But, matters relating to other people's money can be occasionally subject to inconsistent circumstances. You have a deep emotional need for intimate involvement within important relationships. You want to be around important people who can add value to your life. You tend to be responsive sexually, but your emotions can, either be creative or destructive. You will work well with women. You will be good at doing detective or research work, because you know how to probe the unconscious mind. You will be concerned with death and the afterlife.

The Moon in the ninth house:

You have a deeper longing to be motivated and move beyond the mundane and things of life. Because you are a philosophical person, you have an interest in people and different cultures, and you are curious about the world. It is important to have a definite goal in mind, so that you would not be restless and disoriented. There is also a longing to be somewhere else when you are unhappy, which will make you use your imagination to fantasize about traveling and that you are in a happier place. It is important that you avoid the feeling that the grass is greener on the other side.

There is also an indication that you have done excessive traveling in your earlier days. You have a strong desire for things that are far away or foreign, and that you have never experienced before. You are very much concerned with intellectual stimulations to your mind. You will also love to travel and explore other cultures. You can be an excellent teacher, because you understand public attitudes and ideas. However, you can become restless, due to the fact that you have done your fair share of being on the move. You must learn how to expand your horizons, which can be accomplished through travel, and higher education.

The Moon in the tenth house

You have an emotional need for recognition, popularity, achievement and accomplishment. You can be quite charming. When you lead a structured and responsible life, you will be at your emotional best. It is notable that you may change your goals and ambitions, or even your profession frequency, so that you can find the perfect fit. You tend to worry about living up to your own expectations, and that of your family. You make your decisions out of your emotions, or you act on your emotions far too often. There is a challenge setting your heartfelt goals, because it is unlikely that you will find happiness adopting the expectation of others, of which you are sensitive to.

You have an instinct of what the public wants, because you work well with people. There is a strong need for status, which comes through success. Because of your need for accomplishment, you will pursue another career, and while you are climbing the ladder of success, you will change careers, frequently. Consequently, your career may involve working with the public or with women. You are responsive to the outer world, which can be detriment. Your feelings may also be influenced by current events.

The Moon in the eleventh house:

In this position, the Moon shows an emotional need of belonging and feelings; also you will need support from friends and associates. You turn to your acquaintances for support, and offer it in return. If there is an inner emotional unrest, there may be a changeable or unstable social life. You are an individual who is filled with many dreams and hopes for your future. There is a possibility that you will change your goals frequently because of your mood swings. When you are involved in groups, clubs, organizations, community activities, or a network of close friends who support and care for you, this gives you a lot of emotional fulfillment.

Ultimately, you make your friends your family, and you feel a close relationship with those who share the same ideas and beliefs that you hold dear. There is a need for people outside of your family to relate to and belong to. You have a hard time setting goals to work towards and to fulfill them, as a result. You may have many women friends. There is an association with the general public, and you have the ability to be in politics. You tend to feel very protective of your friends, but you need the support that friends and relatives have to offer. There is a need to maintain a certain amount of distance, so that your independence is kept constant. You love to socialize and love popular events.

The Moon in the twelfth house:

There is an emotional attachment and sensitivity to all that is supernatural, groundless, unearthly, and eternal when the Moon is in this position. You are sensitive and this can cause delayed reactions to your own emotional experiences. You need repeated moments of solitude in order to recharge yourself emotionally, and with this need, it can lead to feelings of isolation and of being misunderstood. You are a very sensitive person, and this can cause you to be flooded with emotions that are hard to define, or you may be completely out of touch with what you are feeling.

This will keep you from discovering your emotional needs. If you react to this in a negative manner, you will avoid responsibility, while using hypersensitivity as an excuse for not participating. You are very sympathetic to others, but you are not always emotionally available to offer help. Because your feelings can be a puzzle to you; it is difficult for you to share it with others. You want to care for the oppressed and you want to help them. You are a very imaginative and intuitive person, and you are dreamy and mysterious about your hidden subconscious state of being. You seek peace in secluding yourself from others. You have a strong empathy for the unfortunate, and you want to help humanity. You tend to feel persecuted by others.

Mercury in the first house:

Mercury in a house shows different experiences and the need to communicate and share information. "MERCURY in a house indicates the field of experience which the power to communicate information, to remember the results and causes of past experiences, and to establish relationships. (Rudhyar, 1972, 184) You will be intellectually stimulated, which would help you to adapt and be more alert to your surroundings.

However, people with Mercury in the houses tend to be self-centered. If you have to be preoccupied with the self, you can have nervous tensions, and become too jittery.

You can communicate ideas easily. You view yourself as being different from others, because of your intellectual abilities and how you approach your problems. Self-expression comes easily to you. You are observant, because of your acuity. You relationship with siblings, neighbors, classmates, and friends will become more noticeable, now. You will evaluate the impact that you have on those around you and who you come in contact with. You are motivated to speak about your past. You will have a youthful demeanor; but somewhat mischievous. The way in, which you use your choice of words to attract to get you what you want will work best for you, now.

Mercury in the second house:

"In the second house, there may be need to concentrate intellectually upon financial and managerial problems, or upon ways to make use of the foods for thought provided by one's culture." (Rudhyar, 1972 p. 185) It is important that you learn to manage your money from an intellectual level. You will learn how to do this by learning and identifying with other cultures. When you use your intellectual abilities, you will become more efficient in making money. If you chose to work for someone else, you would need to do something that is active, so that the energy that you have can be used up. You are volatile and can work as an agent, because you know how to use your mental faculties, and you know how to brainstorm without effort.

You will make an excellent writer, manager, or clerk. You are not someone that can be convinced easily nor do you change your mind in a moment's notice. You need to analyze your cash flow, income, and your money making strategies. At this point, you are more practical about your attitude towards finances. This will be a perfect time for you to gather new money making ideas. On the flip side, you tend to worry about your finances. Your conversations are not lighthearted, now: because you will take things more seriously.

Mercury in the third house:

You are attracted to unchanging enterprises that serves the public. You are an individual who has a wealth of ideas that helps to promote your objectives naturally. People in affluential places will be impressed with your mental ability, and they know that your proposals value their attention. "Very good mind if not heavily afflicted. Good for teaching and detailed work. Apt to have an itch to be on the move. Fond of studying and curious about everything." (Hickey, 1972 p. 156) You will have experiences that may be strained, but it must come through the mind, instead of through the emotions.

You can be tied to your relatives, because you worry about them. You are very optimistic when it comes to study and research work. People with Mercury in the third house are fluent and effective speakers, and they love short journeys. Mercury is at home in this house and will offer natural curiosity to the facility with words. You can multi-task, while being on the phone, surfing the net or writing emails. But, there is a possibility that there may be some form of information overload. This can be a busy time with classmates, neighbors and siblings. This is an ideal time to accumulate information from your environment. When circumstances call for you to stick to routine, your mind can be distracted. But, you have an inquisitive mind, and learning tends to be fun for you.

Mercury in the fourth house:

You can have instability in your home environment. This signifies an individual as a homeless wanderer who is constantly moving from place to place. This is a good feature for people who are engaged in an active occupation. However, if you make demands on others, it can cause mental strain, especially if they try to benefit from your talents for their own selfish reasons. But, you normally try not to alternate them, because you may need them in the future. In fact, you will go about your business without interference. You may have anxiety about the home and your domestic affairs.

You tend to be headstrong and can be easily irritated. It is very important that you learn to relax. You have on intellectual concentration, and have personal security and strength of character. The mind is conquered by religious traditions. You have the ability to improve on your concentration. You want solitude, so that you can get some mental work done. You have a rather retentive memory. Discussions about your earlier life and family matters will interest you. Your mind will roam about

69

domestic concerns and issues about the home. People drop by your home very often, or you will take work home.

Mercury in the fifth house:

With Mercury in the fifth house, you have the ability to solve problems very easily. This is one of your best assets, and it will attract favorable attention from supervisors and colleagues. You have well defined goals, and you seek careers that add to what you are worth, as an individual. You have literary abilities and have the capability to scheme your emotional impulses in forms which can communicate them to other people. However, this can cause you to lose your spontaneity and directness. In fact, the mind can also be influenced by ego drives. "Mercury in the fifth House centers the mind upon education, amusements, courtships, and the children.
If Mercury is well aspected by Saturn or Jupiter it gives depth to the mind and makes the person successful in enterprises connected with education, publishing, or public amusements." (Heindel, & Foss Heindel, 1973 p. 196)

Your mind is focused on love affairs in your early life. You tend to have a deep concern for children. You have a powerful mental connection with your creative self-expression. Because you are good at expressing your ideas, you are proud of them. It is easy to entertain others with your conversations. You have a natural sense of humor. You enjoy playing games that requires you to be competitive. There is a strong need for intellectual stimulation. If your partner is an intellectual type, he/she will be appreciated.

Mercury in the sixth house:

You have the tendency to educate yourself, because it does not matter what type of formal training you have. You know how to relay your knowledge to the world, in order to solve problems. This gives you the ability to earn a decent income. It is easy for you to do service. Your thinking habits can be the cost of any ill health, because you tend to worry about what the body needs, so that it can overcome, in order to serve others. Consequently, people who are busy normally do not have the time to think or take care of themselves. It is important that you pay close attention to your diet, and should take vitamins to nourish the body.

You know how to use your intellectual mind when you are at work, also serving a great person. This is the house of self transformation, so the mind should be flexible, in order to bring objectivity to the emotional life of others, also yourself. You feel persuaded to make to do lists. You are the one to have health concerns on your mind. You will spend some of your time researching ways to improve your health. There may be more movement and communication with co-workers, at this time. This is, especially, a good time to do so, because you are objective. It is imperative that you watch out for chit-chat: because it can interfere with your work.

Mercury in the seventh house:

You are definitely prevalent in scientific and literary circles. This is good for people who are public speakers, and all those who are involved in activity of a public nature. You can be sued and would have to defend yourself or you may be libel and have to give account to for your actions. With Mercury in the seventh house, you will have a successful marriage. You enjoy proving that you are more inventive than your competitors. People put their trust in you to handle their financial affairs. When Mercury is in this house, marriage is more of the mind, rather than the emotions.

Your partner is keen and can be very alert. It is also important to overcome bickering and arguments. In fact, it is better for you to settle any difficulties out of court. Another important key is that you must always pay attention to what you sign or put on paper. You are the type to weigh the pros and cons in any situation. There is some indecisiveness because you entertain opposing viewpoints. You are the type that that would spend one to one time people in your inner circle. When you dialogue with others, your thoughts become clearer. You will place a lot of stress on communicating with partners and best friends. Your power of words can be used to advise others and make peace with the people in your life.

Mercury in the eight house:

You tend to be very concerned over your partner's money. Remember to carefully go over all your paperwork. You have the ability to receive an inheritance from a relative, because of death. There may be worry and disagreements with yourself and other individuals who are close to you. You need to go out doors on a regular basis, so that you can get fresh air and oxygen, because you are apt to have trouble with the respiratory system. Also, you should not smoke. However, you should always work out the concrete details of contracts at all levels. You will be in search of things that are beyond, which will give you divine and a greater depth of understanding of the self.

You are very perceptive and will be aware of anyone who tries to demoralize you or if they are being unfair. This is due to the fact that you would make sacrifices for the right individual, because you will do whatever it takes to impress him or her. You are more intuitive now, and can pick up on hidden cues from people that are around you. This is an excellent way of reading between the lines. At this point, you will be excellent at planning and strategizing. You will do well in research. When it comes to approaching sensitive, intimate and personal matters, you will use rational and logic.

Mercury in the ninth house:

You will work to provide the best services, because the public expects this from you. It is important to you that you are the best in whatever you do, and you do this by learning new skills. There is a deep interest in philosophy and higher education. You will have dreams, and vision and you are spiritually empowered. You will want to rule your in-laws, so they would have no control over you. But, in most cases, you should live far away from your in-laws, because it will avoid any misunderstandings. "In the ninth house Mercury is called upon the define as clearly as possible abstract concepts or religious institutions, or to plan carefully distant journeys and large scale attempts at expansion." (Rudhyar, 1972 p. 186)

You have a studious mind and it is easy for you to dig deeply into philosophical problems of life and being. This gives you a broad and flexible mind, and you tend to change how you view things quite frequently. In fact, your mind will turn to bigger ideas, thoughts and vision, at this time; because you are open to expanding your knowledge. You will put everything into perspective rather than labeling. You will have the drive and desire to discuss philosophical things now; since you think about the bigger picture. You can miss your appointments, so be mindful of this.

Mercury in the tenth house:

You display adaptability and you are resourceful, which enables you to cope with the incidences of life. You will make a successful lecturer, writer, or publisher. If you are an air sign, you would have the power of expression. You have the tendency to have many occupations. You will be able to bring an intellectual basis to your calling. This would help to explain your contribution to society and your community. Evidently, you will be drawn to social and professional problems that need to be solved. By doing this, you will be represented and honored for your public standing.

This is the culminating point, which is the midheaven. "Mercury is a reflector a mirror. What it reflects will be shown by its tie up with other planets. Each contact, whether good or ill, is important." (Hickey, 1992 p. 156) At this time, you will think about your career and business matters. You are the type to speak with authority, and you will use the power of your word to influence authority figures. People may turn to you for advice on important matters. You will do some multi-tasking regarding your business, at this time.

Mercury in the eleventh house:

You utilize your thoughts as friends of the mind. But, your friends whether male or female: are normally younger. You may have a hard time avoiding gossiping through the wrong friends. However, you will use the power of your mind to accomplish your goals, which of course: you will use your persistence. You choose to establish contacts with individuals who have an intellectual stature. You should utilize your mind to censure the past, in order to plan for a promising future. Your friends anticipate mental stimulation from you, along with intellectual advice. With this in mind, you articulate clearly your hopes and dreams.

However, your intellect is sharpened and well defined, which gives you an excellent flow of language. Whatever experience you have had with your parents, would have a direct impact on how you build your future. You have a bright and alert mind, and you can come up with innovative ideas. You have a prime interest of sharing your thoughts with others, and they will enjoy your conversations. You are a thinker and stays on tasks, especially with your personal goals and business.

Mercury in the twelfth house:

It is vital that you loosen up, so that you can develop an interest in subjects that have nothing to do with your career. You need to be around people who would help you to forget about your daily routine. You should learn how to go within your mind and meditate to bring balance to your life. Pay close attention to your intuitions and inner voice. Your mind should always be focused on your Karma and subconscious urges. "A subtle mind, secretive, and often aren't able to express itself easily. Interested in occult subjects. Lacks confidence that hides the fact." (Hickey, 1992 p. 157) You will find that your relatives are not on the same level with you, and you are not understood by individuals in your environment.

You have a flair for the mysterious and secret things. You would make a good detective, or on excellent researcher. You are very scientific and would make a good chemist, because you are detailed oriented. People with Mercury in this house have the tendency to have a clouded mind, resulting in insanity. During this cycle, your mind is focused on private matters, and you will not speak out of turn. At this time, you need to do quiet contemplation and meditation. It is also worthwhile for you to examine the past, in order to improve the future, but it is vital for you not to waste your energy on guilty feelings.

Venus in the houses:
Venus in the first house:

You are normally a charming, likable, magnetic, and attractive person: and you tend to wear your feelings on your sleeves it is easy to befriend you, because you are diplomatic and warm in self-expression. You attract others to you quite easily, and you do not come onto people too aggressively. You tend to play dumb, if you are challenged or in doubt. Also, you can be two-faced, due to your passive behavior. If for some reason, you feel that you have given up your power, you may have feelings of resentment. You yearned to be liked by others. Furthermore, you have a way of winning people over to your arguments because off your natural charm and magnetic personality. You love to surround yourself with beautiful things because you have an appreciation for art. You will feel a lack in your life if you do not have a partner, because your love life is important to you.

Venus in the second house:

You have the need for physical expressions of love and affection, because this is important to you. You have an extravagant taste. It is well defined and you are proud of it. Your friends may feel that you have a natural talent to find items of good value and good taste. You have a taste for quality things, and you are very generous, and you give gifts of with expectation of reward. You can be self-indulgent and you are attached to winning admiration from a partner, so that you can find true love. It is highly unlikely that you will jump into a new relationship, and if you do, your feelings will grow gradually.

You yearn for a partner who will make you feel safe and secure. You naturally have strong values, and it is hard for people to move you from this. You are very sensual and touch is appealing to you. It is hard to deny yourself anything. You will allow others to see your soft and receptive self. You will be faced with romantic and pleasure seeking activities, which will come to the forefront. In order to improve your attractiveness, you must pay close attention to your appearance and your mannerisms. Others will agree with you, and this will help them to co-operate with you.

Venus in the third house:

People with Venus in this house of are verbally expressive and diplomatic, and they are very tactful. You know how to win people over with your words. It is easy for you to give out compliments. In some cases, you tend to be genuine, and you may use flattery to your own benefit. You are a good mediator and you aim to settle disputes, so that you can bring peace to the situation. Your need to be sensitive and polite to others doesn't always succeed, because there is a mischievous side to you. It is also very easy for you to engage in mind games. There is a possibility that people may find out that you don't always mean what you say.

You appreciate mental stimulation and you frequently change scenery in your love relationships. Others will find you very cheerful and rather intellectual, during this time. There is an interest of things that you find fascinating and you love to talk about them. The ideas that you are exchanging will be of great value to you. There can be benefit through

75

siblings or in taking short trips. You are a natural mediator and you can solve conflicts.

Venus in the fourth house:

"A love of home and the mother if Venus is not heavily afflicted. There is a lovingness at the roots of being, and the latter part of life will be blessed with happy conditions." (Hickey, 1992 p. 162) Balance is important to you, along with harmony and peace, especially in the home. You are attracted to luxurious and comfortable items in the home. You have an eye for interior decorating. The way you decorate your home shows a loving personal touch. You are sentimental and you show your affection through sympathy and how you nurture others. Normally, you do not give your heart easily but when you do, it is done with great emotion.

Your parenting skills and style is affected by your parent's marriage. In some cases, your parents may be in indulgent and overprotective where you are concerned. You are found of the home and your family. And, on a romantic level, you are more receptive and gentle. You have a love for the aesthetics that are around you, at this point in time. You will do whatever it takes to create a peaceful and stable atmosphere, if things are out of whack. You value loyalty and sensitivity in your relationships. You will find ways to earn money from home. This can bring about a calming influence, and pleasure can be most appealing to you.

Venus in the firth house:

People with Venus in the fifth house are attracted to the opposite sex. They are playful, sensual and passionate. You are in love with love. You blossom on romantic attention. It is actually easy for you to always have a crush or romantic interests. The unmistakable and romantic side of you is due to the fact that you are playful. This keeps you young at heart. Indeed, you are sensual and enjoy the pleasurable senses to the fullest extent. You love to surround yourself with beautiful art and music because these play a role in your ideal date scenario.

You tend to be dramatic when it comes to love and sex. You are loyal to your partner. You are charming and can be easily charmed. It is not hard for you to turn your head. Ironically, you are a warm, fun and playful date. You can turn on the charm without lifting a finger, because

76

Venus is very expressive in this house. You will feel a bit playful now, but your love matters may be touched with a touch of drama. You will have a more loving and appreciative relationship with your children. You are not too aggressive in how you approach love. If you allow yourself to be pursued, you will attract more. You know how to place yourself in the light in order to make a good impression.

Venus in the sixth house:

The way in which you express your love and affection are useful and helpful. You love being helpful to your partner. You are not one to show how you express your love, but you show it by your availability, by serving and doing good things for your loved ones. You will also do thoughtful things. You have talent, especially when it comes to art, because you play attention to every detail. You look for peace and harmony in the system of things. Do not allow yourself to be self-indulgent, because your heart can be affected. "Self-indulgence can affect health if Venus is afflicted in the house. The part of the body afflicted will be shown by the signed Venus occupies." (Hickey, 1992 p. 163)

Be careful that you do not pass up opportunities for love and relationship. This will serve a useful purpose in your life. If you sell yourself short, it will keep you from going after the things you want. You may have romantic activities that evolve around the work environment. You are a well-liked individual and respected on the job. There may be some laziness about you, at this time. You probably would not fall in love for the sake of love.

Venus in the seventh house:

Your life is based on relationship. You do not want to think of being alone. You will not dominate your love, because harmony is important to you. You are definitely the peacemaker, and you go to great lengths to obtain a balanced and harmonious relationship. You have to be very careful not to bend backwards just to keep peace, because you will be taken advantage of. There is a possibility that your partner might be attractive, charming and well off. It is easy for you to magnetically attract people to you, because you have a loving nature. You will contribute to a happy marriage.

You attract love. The things that you give to others eventually will come back to you. Be careful not to enter into partnerships to quickly, because some of your partners can be too shallow. If you use flattery wisely, it will get you everywhere. There is a need to do one to one relating. When you smooth out your relationships, it will make you happy. You will want to get into a committed relationship, if you are single. You are an adaptable individual when it comes to your affections, because you are willing to compromise and negotiate just to make peace.

Venus in the eight house:

You are an individual who seek intensity in your relationships. You do not want casual contact or encounters, because this is not your game. You strive to have drama in your relationships to avoid the boring things of life. You need this because you are easily bored. There is a fear of being vulnerable in your emotions and love. You have a jealous and possessive nature in love because you have a fear of being betrayed. You give yourself wholeheartedly in love and expect total devotion and attention in return. You are a charming person and it runs deeper than the surface.

You have a natural attraction for things that are hidden and mystical. You make your romance something to that of business. A financial boost is possible at this point in time. If you make a deep and intimate connection now, it will help to heal and revitalize you. You will be the first one to smooth over any differences in a partnerships, intimate matters, or other emotionally-charged topics. Your intimate relationships are intensified, because you or your partner wants a deeper union.

Venus in the ninth house:

People of different cultures attract you, and you are attracted to them, as well. And, you are also attracted to a partner who has a sense of adventure. Evidently, you are an individual who expects a certain amount of freedom, especially when you are in a partnership. It is important to you for you to feel that you are growing as an individual, and you do not want to feel confining and restrictive in a relationship. Freedom means a lot to you, because it makes you feel limitless. Your lover must be enthusiastic, and must not be afraid to have a good time with you. You love to travel, and have high ideals for culture.

"Long journeys bring much happiness. Gives a refined and artistic type of consciousness keen appreciation of the higher, cultural aspects of life." (Hickey, 1992 p. 163) You have a taste for the exotics. You do not like routine. Anything that expands your horizons, whether it is physically or mentally, will give you pleasure. You will be attracted to foreign people and places. You are very expansive and generous when it comes to love. The lover that interests you may be someone who you thought would not attract you or someone who have a different cultural background. If you start a romantic relationship at this time, there is a possibility that it can be with someone who has a different educational background.

Venus in the tenth house:

When Venus is in this house, you are charming and people tend to respect you, which is the result of them being drawn to you. You are respected because of this quantity. You have an aura about you that is seen and admired by many. There is a longing for recognition, and admiration for your beauty, charm, or your loving manner. However, it is vital that you do not get caught up with what others think of you. You also have a friendly approach to the world, which will cause you to receive blessings from the world. You naturally attract connections from business and the public, because you have a loving disposition.

Because of this, you may be married to your work or your image. It is easy for you to organize social events. During this time, you are more charming and you are well received on the job. You have likeable qualities when it comes to your responsibilities. You will have opportunities because your reputation will be charming, friendly, and affectionate. Success will come through your goal managerial skills, because you are ambitious. Only the people who are competent will turn your head, at this point in time.

Venus in the eleventh house:

In order for you to sustained romantic interest, the friendship level of your relationships needs to be genuine. You pay close attention to the qualities of the people who you come into contact with, and who you are acquainted with. These are the traits that stands out in people. You are big on setting goals and objectives. You have a lack of discrimination about the friends that you choose. Your relationships must possess eccentric elements in order to keep your interest high. Your calves and ankles as sensitive and can be attractive. One of the ways that you can meet your love is through group activities.

You tend to jump into group affiliation and friendships without thinking about the responsibilities. You are one who would form harmonious friendship that is related to activities within a club, and you may meet someone through this group activity. However, this individual will most likely share your interests; which would make you happy. You may be a bit slightly detached, but you are a very warm individual. If you start a romantic relationship, it would be built on strong feelings of comradeship. This will make it lack deep feelings of intimacy.

Venus in the twelfth house:

Because you are big on romance, you tend to live and breathe your partner once you are hooked. You are not very good at defining your boundaries where your partner's needs are separated from your needs. Due to this, you can get hurt in love easily, and you can feel used quite easily. It is easy for you to be attracted to people from all walks of life. Be careful not to get a partner who would take advantage of you. It is not always safe to be openly affectionate and trusting. There is a chance that you may get involved in a secret love affair or you may fall in love with someone who is not available.

"Sometimes there is a hidden love of fear not known to others. If afflicted by Neptune the person may be in love with someone who was not free." (Hickey, 1992 p. 164) Love and sacrifice seems to go hand in hand for you. You will give up something just to be with the one you love. Evidently, at this time, you would hibernate into your private place, so that you can regroup yourself. You express yourself behind closed doors, and this will be a good time for endings. At this time, you will have secretive contacts with some people; or even have secret love affairs. Because you tend to be shy, you may have romantic frustration.

Mars in the houses:
Mars in the first house:

You react immediately to new situations in a pressing manner, because you are an active, dynamic, energetic, or even forceful and aggressive person. You possess the ability to begin new endeavors with zest. But, you may not be the individual to follow through on things. "This

80

position of Mars causes the personality to throw itself into whatever it wishes to do. Intense activity is necessary if this energy is to be used constructively." (Hickey 1992 p. 169) When Mars is in the first House, some individuals may have an inconsiderate nature, or they may be overly assertive.

You are very independent and you are direct and straightforward. You are a good organizer and you are very confident and self-reliant, but you have the tendency to stir up trouble. It is; however, easy for you to stand your ground and affirm yourself, during Mars transit. You have a lot of energy to move your plans forward; because it is important to you that you leave your mark on the world. You tend to have a short temper, because you are a bit combative, due to a short temper. In the midst of you taking charge of your life, you do not bulldoze over others. You have physical vitality and you are very assertive.

Mars in the second house:

You are definitely a hard worker, but you can be a bit slower than others because you focus on one method. You have a love to produce things of real value. You are very ambitious when it comes to making money and acquiring possessions. However, you have the tendency to be impatient or impulsive, when comes to spending money. You are possessive when it comes to people and material things. Because you like to work independently, it is important for you to achieve things on your own, and you defend your values passionately. As a child, you never liked being rushed to do anything, because you liked to achieve good results, you would have had a focused attention span.

Children with Mars in the second house would be great at saving pocket money. However, these children may not be selfish, but they will want to share on their own terms. Do not get into any impulsive buying, so avoid using credit: simply because: your spending habits may be excessive. However, you may have a lot of energy to make money. This is a very resourceful time, but you must make the most of what you have. At this time, you will have energy for new money making projects. In your efforts to reach to the top of the game, you may try to prove yourself to others. If there are any conflicts, it is likely to be issues of ownership.

Mars in the third house:

At times, you tend to shoot from the hips when it comes to expressing your ideas and opinions, because you speak your mind readily. You have knowledge of a variety of subjects and you love to share your knowledge with others, and at times: you lend to it a bit forcefully. This is because you are clear and direct when it comes to communicating. You tend to get a bit agitated about what others may think is trivial, and you love a good debate. You would make a good politician. You have good skills when it comes to winning things manually, but it is in your nature to become impatient with tasks.

When you are expressing yourself, you tend to be animated, enthusiastic, and energetic. You will defend your family and your childhood. At this time, you can channel your energy on working on intellectual task, but you must do this with passion. You will have many ideas and plans, but be careful not to scatter your energies, as a result of this. You will definitely be busy running errands and communicating with others; and your communicative style will be assertive, because you will be more lucid, at this time. Do not take things personally right now, because your discussions can escalate into heated arguments.

Mars in the fourth house:

You are aggressively protective of your family and close friends. Your anger may be deeply buried and felt, which will cause it hard for others to uncover your true motives. You have the tendency to be a passive aggressor in your approach, and this can lead to resentment, if you are not careful. You have to make a direct if you want to get what you want in life. Family energies are lively and often intense, and you may have arguments with them, or on their behalf. Also, you would have a lot of energy to do domestic projects and activities. Your actions; however, are often ruled by your instincts, and of course, you do not like to be manipulated or forced into doing anything that you don't feel in your guts.

You are the type that would rule the home, and you take on leadership at home and with family. You govern your actions by your instincts, and you may be overly defensive, which can cause you to get over worked up about old angers regarding any emotional issues over the past. All this can be due to the fact that you are restless and moody. Your desire to rule the roost can be family related. You would probably have arguments about them, but on their behalf. Some things may resurface and it can be regarding emotional issues.

Mars in the fifth house:

"This energizes the drive for creative self-expression. The first house is the release of power; the compulsion to express yourself." (Hickey, 1992 p. 169) You have a strong love for love and pleasure, and you pursue romance directly. Most of you are sports lovers, and enjoy anything that has an element of risk appeals or entertains you. You will put a lot of energy in pursuing entertainment, satisfaction and games. You are playful and demonstrated, and you can enjoy putting on a show. You are very competitive, and your children may have children that are boisterous. You are most often, open and affectionate.

You charm people into getting your own way, and people tend to forgive you quite easily. You would do well in sports that need to use physical activities. Your friends admire you, but relationships may suffer because you change partners often. You will have self-discipline, along with your self-expressive energy. You can channel this energy into creative ideas, romantic activities, activities with your children, and sports. This is a passionate time for you; because your romantic life is stepped up a notch. You are the type to put more energy into pleasure and play. Do not burn the candle at both ends.

Mars in the sixth house:

You would work yourself to the point of exhaustion, because you are naturally a hard worker, and you put a lot of energy into your work. You would do best working for yourself instead of working for others, because you tend to become impatient. This happens when members of the team are not working at the same paste like you. When people procrastinate, this upsets you. What it come to organizing and reorganizing, classifying, sorting and analyzing, you know how to apply yourself when doing these tasks. When anyone criticizes or intrude upon the work that you do, you can easily become defensive.

You always do your best with any project, because you identify with it personally, because you expect your coworkers to be enthusiastic with the way you are about it, and put in the same effort. You demand credit for the work that you do, but you may have a larger work load. You have a burst of energy to do your daily routine. You should take charge of your health. At this time, you need to work with your coworkers in a more harmonious manner, so that you can avoid any disputes. In order to channel your energies in a positive and productive manner, you need to find projects that you love doing, but the ones that would bring out your creativity.

Mars in the seventh house:

People with Mars in the seventh house may enter into marriage at an early age, and may do it without thinking about it, and may experience conflict in a marriage that is not working. You may experience legal difficulties. At times, in partnerships, you may have trouble in business. It is easy for you to settle any difficulties out of court. You have sexual energy, and you need a partner who is willing to challenge you, which is someone who holds his or her own arguments. There is a source of conflict in your life with your close relationships. You partners bring out the aggressive side of you.

It is very important for you to cultivate the art of compromise if you want peace in your love life and relationship. You must avoid jumping into altercations with others. You must not allow your partnerships to suffer because of conflicts. Instead, use your energy to work cooperatively on any problems with relationships, which will make your relationships energetic and dynamic. When any differences arise, you are the first one to settle it. You are not the one to sweep things under the rug.

Mars in the eight house:

People with Mars in this house have strong desires and when you decide to possess something, you succeed in doing so. There is a possibility that you may experience shortage in love or money. This would encourage you to be less possessive in these areas of your life. You have the ability to see through the false pretense of others. You can make up for past lives, because of your Karma. There is a possibility that there may be sexual trauma in your early life, and you may struggle with this as an adult. However, you may not experience true love until later in life, but when you do, it is magical.

You fear being betrayed by others. "Misuse of psychic power in a past lifetime could lead to obsession and psychic difficulties." (Hickey, 1992) Your sexuality is stimulated, at this point in time. There is a possibility that you may experience conflicts over possessions with your partner. This may be a time of endings for you. You may hear things that may, either touch or disturb you. You are very strategic in your actions and you are aware of any intricacies of human interaction. Your best course of action is to realize that you can rely on others for support.

Mars in the ninth house:

You love long distance traveling. There may be conflict with in-laws so it is best to live at a distance away from them. You are a very independent person and you are an enthusiastic individual. Be careful that your religious beliefs do not lead you to fanaticism. You are an open-minded individual, and you love the challenge of the debate. Avoid being self-righteous and disregard the opinion of others to uncover truths. Sexually, you are playful and energetic, and it is a sport to you. You are honest and at times, you are downright blunt. People find your sense of humor and direct approach attractive.

Your lasting impression attracts others and your zest for life is unmistakable. You naturally love people that make you laugh, and they will have something interesting to say about your life. You are energetic and more bold than usual. You are restless and have a deep hunger for adventure, which would be expressed, at this time. You will find ways to expand your activities, but at the same time: you want to increase your level of education, travel or for new subjects.

Mars in the tenth house:

Children with Mars in the tenth house do not need to be coaxed, and are born wanting to succeed in life. And, success will come to them, and from an early age. Also, they will know that in order to get to where they want to go in life, they have to work hard at accomplishing that. They set goals early in life, and they will push to reach those goals. This child will be more serious than most children, but the fear is also a strong need to be respected by your peers. While they are young, their eyes will be set on the future. Popularity is not important to them. But, they would want to be recognized as being smart or cute.

It is important that the child learns how to be compromising because when he or she becomes an adult, this attitude will be taken to the job place. There may be some friction with your father, and you may separate from him by choice. Your ambition to be recognized for your accomplishments is stimulated. You, indeed, have a desire for others to notice you, professionally or otherwise. During this time, you will become more self-empowered, which can give you the initiative to start a business.

Mars in the eleventh house:

Your "energy is strongly directed towards achieving goals and objectives. Important to seek the right kind of friendships for the wrong reasons can bring plenty of difficulties." (Hickey, 1992 p. 170) You will use her talents to work with people to achieve your personal goals. There is a great possibility that you would have few close friends because you are busy enlarging your circle, so that you can have many permanent relationships. You do not have the innate ability to be a team player, but you will grow to understand that support is necessary to further your ambitions. It is imperative for you to understand how to take caution; you have to learn to say "no".

By getting involved in group activities or cooperative efforts, you stand a better chance of achieving your goals. At this point, you will have a lot of ideas of what you want to do and how you are going to do it. Do not allow your ego to dominate others. You are the type who will want to lead the group, rather than following, but you can find ways of doing this without stepping on the toes of others. When you work as a team, you will accomplish your goals, rather quickly. You can do this by networking. You have a keen humanitarian impulse, and it can be stimulated, during this time.

Mars in the twelfth house:

When you were a child, you may have been afraid to affirm yourself. You would have felt defeated before you start anything. If you are around people who did not encourage you, you would have express feelings of tiredness. Your self-confidence would need to be built on your courage to disregard anyone that tries to inflict negativity in you. Children tend to work in secret and act behind peoples' backs. But, as a child you may have been blamed for things that you did not do. As an adult, you then come off as being mild, but if you are pushed you can be a difficult foe.

You are intelligent, and you can give forceful emotional restriction, which can be hard to suppress. You have a feeling of dependency on yourself, because you can have false accusations from your enemies. While reflecting on your goals, you need to do some research so that everything will find its rightful place. The actions of the past will certainly catch up with you. Channel your energies into taking care of private matters, privately. Your unconscious behavior patterns may have an influence on the way that you assert yourself. Most of you will enjoy an active dreaming life, and their imagination can serve them well.

Jupiter in the houses:
Jupiter in the first house:

Jupiter in the first House signifies expansion around travel, and people within their first house tend to be overweight. In the material world, you normally give abundance two things that please you. This can give you reasons to be self-indulgent. You have to be careful that you do not give way to egotism or hypocrisy. You have interest in sports and you will do very well in them. You have the ability to be a CEO of a company, or your own businesses. You will make an excellent board member, and you will do well in your company, and with groups of people. When you are presenting yourself to the world around you, you do it in a jovial, kind, and altruistic manner.

Your faith does not lack optimism. You have a pure belief in positive thinking. You have strong morals, and you are a principled person. There will be noticeable movements in your environment and with your self-confidence. This is a good time to be expansive, energetic, and enthusiastic about your goals and desires. This will boost your optimism and generosity. You will greet life with a can do attitude. You will leave the things of the past in the past and focus on the future, so that you can welcome life with a fresh attitude. You will not sweat the small stuff. It is important to you that you make a distinct first impression on the people that you meet. You have a confident attitude that the sky is the limit and you can achieve all of your goals.

Jupiter in the second house:

You know how to attract resources and money easily. You are confident, but you have the tendency to be extravagant, and you may spend all of your money. Because of this, it is important for you to learn money-management skills. You would do well in banking or dealing with stocks and bonds. Also, you will do very well as a salesperson. You are a resourceful individual, and you can be perceived as being lucky with money, by your peers. You would not have a problem getting gifts or attracting personal possessions. Your love comfort and your five senses are very acute.

You can become overindulgent in material things. You have a strong image of yourself and want others to view you in a professional manner, because you want to make an impression on others. Your value system, especially when your possessions are heightened. You can have a very productive year with Jupiter in this house, but your self-confidence must be in check in order for you to boost your earning power. By doing this, your income will be increased, and you will have opportunities to improve your financial situation. There is a strong possibility that you may receive a large gift or bonus. You will pay close attention to who you are and your self-worth.

Jupiter in the third house:

You are definitely a likable and optimistic individual. As a child growing up, you would have been very happy, which is beneficial to your well-being and confidence. You have a good relationship with immediate and extended family, which would be beneficial for you when you are forming relationships with your brothers and sisters. Your mental power and intuition is very strong. It is important to do an occupation that keeps you mentally stimulated. You know how to plan carefully. You enjoy making happy connections with others because you are very curious. You love to share ideas with others and you take pleasure in doing so, because this is important to you.

You possess the ability to see the bigger picture, and often: people turn to you for advice. You have a sincere interest in others, and it is easy for you to put them at ease. You are a trustworthy individual. There will be opportunities for you to further your education, during this time. You will learn how to disseminate this knowledge, by expressing your ideas in a productive manner. There will be opportunities for you to travel, and this venture will help you to expand your mind. You are very sociable and others appreciate this quality in you. You have the ability to write and author books, because you are most creative when you do this.

Jupiter in the fourth house:

You are generally an openhearted person, and you are generous. In your place of birth, you would have success. You will gain a lot through your parents and through inheritance. You must live in a comfortable home, and you do not like clutter in the home because you like space. You would experience happiness at a later time in life. However, you are guided by your strong instincts, especially on a professional level. You enthusiastically make warm connections with others. In old age, it is expected to be pleasant and rewarding. There were strong morals that were reinforced in your childhood.

Your dream is to attain a large spacious home and you usually get this. One of your feelings is that happiness is home. You will see benefits in the home, property, family, and domestic matters. You will find joy and enjoyment in the family, because you will have a deeper sense of security. You yearn for stability, so that you can achieve inner peace and contentment. At this time, you may either buy or sell a house, or have an addition to the family. You love to live in a spacious home, so this may be the time to move to that larger home. You will ignore any long lasting family problems, especially if they were with your parents. Also, you may receive financial support from your parents.

Jupiter in the fifth house:

You are naturally a generous, playful and one warm individual, especially with children and in your romantic life. You can be prosperous by using your creativity, in areas that deals with entertainment, recreation and children. You are very talented at teaching, because you know how to show patience and love for the learning process and the students that you are teaching. You most definitely love sports and having good times. "If unafflicted, extremely creative and much success and happiness through children of the imagination as well children of the body." (Hickey, 1992 p. 174) You will find gain through investments, and can make a good investment advisor.

Jupiter in the sixth house:

89

You set and have high standards, in your business ventures and dealing with people. You believe that one should always treat others with respect. By doing this, you may miss out on business opportunities. However, others tend to build faith in your honest approach in the long run. You are a philanthropist and would help those who are less fortunate than you. It is very important that you pay close attention to your diet because rich foods will attract you and this may cause problems in your life. You take great pleasure in the work that you do, and you love to be useful to others. You love to serve, and you would have productive relationships with the quickest. You are loyal to your employer. You may have trouble with your health.

Jupiter in the seventh house:

You will cultivate your close partnerships, which is important to you. You are very talented when it comes to negotiating, and you like fair play. You are excellent when it comes to mediating on behalf of others. You will be fortunate with legal matters. You will succeed best in partnerships and relationships because you value people. You will use charm and grace to reach your goals. You are sociable and very good-natured and will attract beneficial partnerships. You may marry more than one time, and you may have material gain through marriage. There is a chance that you may marry someone who was been married before

Jupiter in the eight house:

You are very talented at strategizing in research and investigation. You have the ability to get to the root of every problem, and you instinctively feel that this is where the answer lies. You certainly take pleasure in unraveling the mysteries and solving problems. You get to a partner emotionally and materially. Taboos do not shock you. You gain money through partners and through inheritance. If you do not pay attention, you can become extravagant: and you will not have good judgment. You are a very emotional individual and it is important that you weigh things and conditions carefully, before you take action. You have strong sexual drives.

Jupiter in the ninth house:

People with Jupiter in the ninth house have a hunger for knowledge and wisdom. You are a naturally philosophical individual, and you love sharing your opinion and knowledge with others. You have a

90

natural ability to teach and you love the learning process. You value freedom of movement and love to express yourself while you are teaching. You know how to be an inspirational and well-traveled individual. You can publish books and journals. You love foreign cultures. Furthermore, you have a deep interest in religion, and you would have travel and expansion through it. You would have success in obtaining higher education and writing, so that you can publish. Your in-laws can be a source of pleasure. You have good judgment and an acute intuition. You may have a love for living in foreign countries.

Jupiter in the tenth house:

You take charge easily, when you use a winning kind approach, while doing so. People see you as lucky when it comes to your career and business opportunities. It is natural for you to excel. If others help you along the way, it would be due to your winning attitude. You are mature, ethical, and resourceful. You value achievement and you love to manifest, as well as those who take responsibility for their lives. Position can be quite important to you as well as your status. "Great desire for achievement. Attracts others and great success through profession. Career usually one that entails service to those limited and afflicted." (Hickey, 1992 p.175) You can work in the medical field. You have expansive appearance that attracts others to you. You set a high moral standard.

Jupiter in eleventh house:

People love their social life and it means a lot to them, and they take pleasure in connecting with their friends and the environment you are a team player and you will be involved in your community. There is a great deal of benefit through friends who are influential. You are selfless by nature and you value your personal freedom. You are open to new systems and you are a tolerant individual, which is why you are a humanitarian. You love friends who achieve their goals in life. You may also attract the wrong friends, which may cause you downfall in life. You can have benefits through travels.

Jupiter in the twelfth house:

You are definitely considered the Guardian angel, but you can be saved in the nick of time. This is due to your inborn faith with the universe. You love solitude and love working alone. Meditation will give you pleasure, peace and rejuvenation. You are a merciful and gracious

91

person, and you often give anonymously. People may call you the invisible protector. You should work in medical institutions and you will do well in doing research. You also like working behind the scenes. You love your privacy. It is important to that you do not do things in haste, because it can hurt your chance of success. You can make poor judgment. You stand to gain through your enemies, directly or indirectly: but they can turn into your friend, in the end.

Saturn in the houses:
Saturn in the first house:

As Saturn positions itself in the first House, it demonstrates how the individual projects heads on her personal energies with others. The individual's personality is being defined in a fundamental way. You may have a stern exterior, and you look differently when you smile, and still exterior drops. You are more aware than others. And, if the people around you are demanding, they will dominate your consciousness, and it may be a bit difficult for you to place yourself ahead of others. You may feel guilty about things that other people think are insignificant. You tend to be hard on yourself. It is important that you think things through by yourself or with someone you feel comfortable with, so that you can fight the guilt.

Saturn in the second house:

The presence of Saturn in the second house signifies that some people may experience difficulty of obtaining real-world possessions like money, cars, etc. This will help to reflect the individual's attitude towards possessions. You may be pessimistic about your own ability to get possessions. However, you may be overly cautious in the way that you do investments, especially your finances. For example, you only invest in your hard earned money in lower risk of treasury bonds, instead of the stock market. And, it may be good or bad. Your investments would remain rock solid over the years, and they would not grow as much as if you were a risk taker. Awareness of this attitude can be your strength.

Saturn in the third house:

Since the third house deals with the unconscious operating of the mine, it indicates that natural way in which you act and communicate with people. It is easier for you to review the way in which your mind works in any circumstances. But in this sense, it is conscious. You may feel ill at ease when you go about your day to day routine. Some of you may come across as being cold and reserved, and you may have a few words to say, which of course can turn someone off. But this can be used to your advantage to listen to other people, so you would not have to do much of the talking. You have a serious mind, and you can concentrate easily. You have the tendency to separate yourself from your relatives and have no connection to them. You are a good student, and you will go to school for life. It is not a good idea for you to smoke because the lungs aren't strong.

Saturn in the fourth house:

This house indicates the way you relate to your family, as a child and adult. It shows your attitude to giving and receiving, whether you will mother or nurture others. However, with Saturn in this house: it can limit the nurturing that you are capable of, but this may come off as being cold or impersonal. This is due to the fact that you may perceive your childhood as being one that lacked warmth and affection. You would take on responsibility at an early age, because you will feel that you are making up for being neglected as a child. But, with Saturn in this house, it takes away the fun of nurturing and makes it a chore, but this can be extended to the community, hometown, and country. You are patriotic and loyal. You may receive an inheritance. You will find happiness in the later part of your life.

Saturn in the fifth house:

You love to play and express yourself. You are a spontaneous person, but you have to be careful. You may be viewed as the party pooper, or even a bad date. You must avoid this from happening to you. However, you may find that you make excuses, when it comes to having fun. You are the all work and no play kind of person, but you don't need to make any excuses to have fun and enjoy life. It is easy for you to get into an activity that deals with raising money for a good cause, which can be turned into a fun occasion. When you are dating, you can allow your date to lead a bit, but if your date did have the same fifth house, Saturn: then you have nothing to worry about.

Saturn in the sixth house:

When Saturn is in the sixth house, you would have "success in work that deals in service to others. Good relationships with employees as a fellow worker have. Is a loyal worker and dependable." (Hickey, 1992 p. 175) This is the house where Saturn is most comfortable and it also rules your attitude about work, service, and your body. You may also experience self-denial, because you put off pleasing yourself. You will pursue activities to please others for another purpose. One of the examples that you will set is working to make a living, and you do it as a sense of responsibility not to please yourself. You are a workaholic, and you may find yourself living to work, and it is important to avoid this! You have a strong sense of responsibility to work and you take service seriously.

Saturn in the seventh house:

This is the house that rules partnerships and marriages. It also would reveal how you relate to your closest friends and partner. Because it opposes the first house, which signifies the way you project your energies towards others. And the seventh house signifies the energies you project onto others, and the energies that you are looking for in a relationship. This is part of your own energies. Successful marriages are connected to this house. There are a number of things that is connected to this house when Saturn finds home near. You may have few relationships, or you may feel weighed down by a sense of responsibility and this may turn off relationships, because of this. It might be difficult to build bridges without someone else, and it may keep you away from building new relationships. You take relationships more seriously than others.

Saturn in the eight house:

Saturn in the eighth house shows that someone can die a horrible death. It can also be known as the house of resurrection. You will experience transformation through growth and change. You would need to reinvent yourself from time to time. You have to pay close attention to how you feel about possessions. Your attitude about reminders of the past is to let it go and move on: making the necessary changes. You can have a powerful influence on others, and you can resist change, if you are not careful. You are set in your ways, and changes can be stressful for you causing you to worry. You must be prepared for change, and you would want to chart out an action plan when you are about to make changes. Changes can make your life better.

Saturn in the ninth house:

You are a philosophical person, and you know how to rationalize your conscious mind. Saturn in this house shows that you will know how to govern the functions of your higher mind. The thought process that defines you as a human and your mind is always expanding. It also helps to define your personal philosophy of life and your perception of life. The way you react to new ideas depends on how you perceive things, because you are a practical minded person. You are not the one to fantasize. In one way or the other, you are closed to new ideas. It is not a good idea for you to dismiss ideas too quickly. Your assets are that you can be practical in your thinking.

Saturn in the tenth house:

You are positioned for success and prosperity, and you would have a desire to achieve things. In your profession, you will attract honors and success to you, and it would be done where you serve, and you would do well in the medical field and working with people. You set high moral standards and you will attract a position of importance in your life. You will be able to identify with the work that you choose. Men would be able to identify with their fathering role, and they take it seriously. Fathers would be concerned with the development of their children in the real-world. You are a natural born leader. You take things very seriously. Your leadership style is based on practical aspects of life. You know your role in life, but you can become very defensive about things. You can take on responsibilities with ease, but you must learn to delegate some.

Saturn in the eleventh house:

Saturn in the eleventh house governs the functions, the one to many relationships, with friends, family, and organization that you work for. You may tend to think that socializing is tiresome, and you may want to stay alone. You will feel uncomfortable and self-conscious about going through the motion. If you are doing anything with a group, you will be afraid to fail, because you don't want to be ordinary or just a part of the crowd. Because you take friendships seriously, you may have a fear of forming friendships. You may think that they will burden or obligate you. However, there may be a feeling of loneliness. You need to take time to personalize social interactions. You need to develop a few good friends to hang out with you, because you have a great capacity to be loyal.

Saturn in the twelfth house:

You may deny energies that exist. You may have an early life setback, which will prompt you to push realities into the unconscious. You are an individual who is plagued with guilt, and it can be difficult for you to know where it is coming from. You may have anxieties that you cannot define. However, the source of the anxieties may come from fear of the unknown. You may have a hard time submitting to the idea that you need help from others, and you would withdraw from others and try to handle the problems for yourself. When your innermost feelings are exposed, you tend to feel vulnerable and dependent on others. It is very important for you to learn how to embrace your sorrows and be freed from guilt, so that you can get to a place of true self- acceptance.

Uranus in the houses:
Uranus in the first house:

In this position, Uranus alters the way in which the individual projects his or her personal energies unto others. You may seek freedom or demand the way you present yourself to the world. You will dress simply, but strangely, and you would have no problems in asserting yourself. You are, most definitely, not shy in letting everyone know where you stand on issues. When you present your unique perspective, you take pride in it. You are a unique soul with few demands, wants and needs, and you tell yourself this. You feel a sense of selflessness and you want to change the world. Your relatives and friends may find you a bit unreasonable at times, which does not bother you in the least, because you know how to be good hearted, and genuine about your feelings. You lose interest quickly, because your passion rises fast.

Uranus in the second house:

The way you view real-world possession differs from most, and you see to look at money, cars and other possessions as a means to an end. But, if this satisfies your personal needs or your heart's desires, then you are authorized to have some of your own. But, you do not want these things to tie you down to one place, and hence you will need your freedom. However, if you feel tied down, then you will shy away from achieving worldly possessions. The possessions that you seek will be ones that help you lead the free lifestyle that you so desire. And, you may also value money in the bank as money that can buy you the freedom that you crave. This is why you have "ups and downs in money conditions. Not a fixed income. Great desire for independence to do well in their own business." (Hickey, 1992 p. 188)

Uranus in the third house:

You have to learn how to accept your environment in your early years, but if you are rebellious, this can cause difficulties. If you have had a rough and painful childhood, it can affect you in later life. You have the innate ability to be a chemist or a scientist who is interested in research. You know how to act and communicate with people around you in a passionate way, and you know how to make people smile, because of your sense of humor. People normally look at you to ease a boring day knowing that you would have something to say about the everyday things of life. Your oddity may puzzle and sometimes annoy some of your friends, but you win them over with your humble nature, and your honesty. You are creative in the way that you communicate.

Uranus in the fourth:

When Uranus is in the fourth house, this may alter your nurturing style. You are the type to seek unusual ways to express your hopes and desires; this is a quality that sets you apart from most people. The concept of nurturing doesn't really come very easy to you. Because of your independent streak, you may want to run away from nurturing if it is offered to you, but you are nurturing, loving, and caring. At times, you prefer to be alone. You may appear selfish to others, but there isn't anything wrong with your intentions, because you normally have the best intentions. Also, with Uranus in the fourth house, it represents the mothering that you have received as well, and you will remember your childhood as satisfactory in material areas, but lacking in emotional support.

Uranus in the fifth house:

You love to play and express yourself as a happy individual. You love to create, and change is something that you can adapt to easily. You are the one that takes great pleasure in doing things differently. Because you are naturally creative, it is easier for you to implement change. When you were a teenager, or as a teenager you would have wanted to date an older person. And, in your love relationships, it always starts off with a twist. You are charming in love, and you will create your own world with ease. You love freedom which will make you choose activities that would sound weird to others. Interesting, you will go about life with spunk and find challenges in almost everything that you do. Your offbeat lifestyle is stimulating to others.

Uranus in the sixth house:

People with Uranus in the sixth house are good workers and they are very independent. Your job must allow you to move around. You do not like routine. You have a brilliant mind, and you are original. You are the type who will learn the hard way in order to be obedient. You love work that has to deal with science and technology. You love freedom on the job, so you will look for a job that offers you that. You are not the type to work on a 9-to-5 job, because it will turn you off. Your work desk will always be messy. You like doing ordinary things in an efficient way. You will keep up with the changing views of health experts, because of your views on health. You do things to sort yourself, because you don't go with the norm.

Uranus in the seventh house:

Your partner may complain about your careless behavior. He or she tends to think that you are inconsistent, but will be charmed by your genuineness and your simplicity. There is reason that you may shy away from making a commitment, and may not see relationship as something that is truly good. This is due to your freedom loving way, which will make you feel tied down. When you chose your mate, you will look for someone who doesn't mind being alone, because your perfect partner would love freedom as much as you do. Because of this, you may have difficulty in marriage, and you may go through divorce or separation. You would need a great deal of discipline in this area and in partnerships.

Uranus in the eight house:

You have a strong and clear intuition. You have to be careful with business partners, and you must think things through before you enter into any partnerships. You may experience difficulties with inheritance, but you may come into a windfall of blessings. It is important to control your sexual pleasures. Your bad temper may cause accidents, so do not do drive when you are angry. In this house of resurrection, Uranus is at home. You are an open-minded individual and you are open to change. You view it as good. You have to reinvent yourself, from time to time. For you, life would be boring without change. The way in which you bring about change leaves people breathless. No one doubts your good intentions. You can; however, overlook human emotions, because you are addicted to your own ideas. You do not go with the status quo.

Uranus in the ninth house:

People would be comfortable with new ideas when Uranus is in this house, and they are not traditional. You have a passion to play around with new ideas. You love to travel and meet new people, reading anything that involves expanding the mind will stimulate you. People who are too conservative might turn you off. Activities that call for higher thinking is an opportunity for you to add your unique creative spin to them. Your natural instincts would help you to accept or reject the boundaries of the world, and you will constantly keep looking for opportunities to expand any limits that the world has placed on you. You would have "success in publishing, technology, or in foreign affairs. Gives unusual journey, either on material plane or unusual experiences where does super conscious planes are concerned." (Hickey, 1992 190)

Uranus in the tenth house:

You definitely do not conform, and you have the need to be your own boss. You love to give and you are a natural humanitarian. You have on originality to your personality which is part of your imagination. Once you make up your mind about something, it is difficult to persuade you otherwise, because you are very independent. You don't want to be described by one thing that you do. You are, most definitely, always on the move in your career, and you don't wish to be identified with only one, and you are a competent individual. One of the things that you do best is maintain your identity. You do not strive for social status. Men would make an excellent father and they can be quite unconventional.

Uranus in the eleventh house:

Because you are too independent, it is difficult for you to identify with a group. But, when it comes to your goals and ambitions, you are independent about them. You are not the one to compromise to fit in with others. However, you tend to feel a bit superior to people who do that. You have a personal charm, and with that, it can mesmerize many. When you are interacting in a group, you may come across as being unfriendly or erratic, and this can cause misunderstandings with the members of the group. However, people would appreciate you for your simplicity and honesty. At times, you would rather be alone in a quiet place. But you will connect well with people who share your principles, and you will build lasting relationships with them. You will make unpredictable changes to your goals, and you will change your mind a number of times, before you decide what you want to do.

Uranus in the twelfth house:

When Uranus is in the twelfth house, people feel the need for freedom and a noble desire to change the world. This is something that they hold deep on the inside and it means a lot to them. However, if you are a successful businessman/woman, you are likely to start an organization that would encourage entrepreneurs. You will seek personal freedom, and help to make the world a better place. In your close relationships, you look for individuals who love freedom and creativity. Careers in science and technology will suit you well, and you may be very artistic and creative, as well. In everything that you do, you will be drawn to surpass all the limits that are placed by the world and society.

Neptune in the houses:
Neptune in the first house:

You have the ability to express yourself artistically, and you may come across as gently, sensitive, and dreamy. You are very sensitive to the environment. People tend to say what they want to see in you, but this does not alter or deter you in any way. You are generally a peace loving person. You do not come on strong, but you can be elusive, alluring and intriguing. People will feel that you understand them and they would be drawn to you, due to this. There is a strong chance that you can be moody and your first reaction to problems might be that you want to escape or feel sorry for yourself. You may struggle with your impressionability, because you may not feel a strong sense of identity. You absorb the moods off others like a sponge. You have a powerful imagination, and you have an easy-going manner.

Neptune in the second house:

You don't like attaching too much value on money, and if you overdo this, you may experience quite a few problems concerning money and ownership. There is a possibility that you can make money through artistic pursuits. However, it is important that you avoid any potential pitfalls of putting too much faith on ideas that you do not have enough grounding in reality. It is; therefore, important that you seek financial advice because you are not a materialistic, which may lead to impartial attitude towards money. Furthermore, when it comes to making money, you act on hunches and intuitions. Your faith is: that you will come into money, one day, or you may day dream about being wealthy. But, you must have faith in your own self-worth; however, if you feel as wealthy as you wish to be, then faith will bring you exactly what you desire.

Neptune in the third house:

The dry cold facts are hard for you to absorb, and traditional teachings might not appeal to you. But, of course, you are talented at visualizing, a different way of learning. You are very perceptive and have the ability to dream, but you can get your head in the clouds and miss the important duties. Consequently, you would have problems with communicating tending to errands, sticking to schedules, and the daily activities. When you hear specific directions, you may turn out, and miss helpful and important details. You may miss or be late for appointments. You seem to intuitively understand people and you can put them at ease in your communication. Because of your charm, you express yourself creatively and imaginatively. You may encourage misunderstandings without knowing it because you are rarely definite in what you say. When you were younger, learning could have been a bit challenging, because you probably have lacked discipline and you found it difficult to gain interest.

Neptune in the fourth house:

There may have been an absent or preoccupied parent figure in your life when you were a child, and your childhood may have been complexed. There may have been chaos in your early home lifestyle, and you may have had difficulties in finding your identity and your groundedness, because of this. You may have longed for a stronger sense of mothering, nurturing, and family in your home life. Because of this, you may create an extended family, including nonfamily, which would help you to feel loved and nurtured. For women, this would help them to feel as a mother figure giving themselves freely to others. It is important to set some limits. You will feel the need to escape into a quiet place in order to refill your spirit. When others overwhelm you, you might isolate yourself from them, regardless. However, you strive to see family clearly.

Neptune in the fifth house:

Your strong sense of drama contributes to your imaginative and creative side. You feel inspired by art and this gives you the feelings to

101

express yourself in a dramatic manner. This will make you an excellent actor. Also, you can be a creative teacher or caregiver who is drawn to children with special needs. You have a strong need to be appreciated, especially in romantic relationships. In your love life, there are a lot of fantasies, and your need for drama may make you see what is not there, and your romantic perception may not be accurate. Interesting enough, you may attract chaotic, unusual, and secretive circumstances in your life, if you are not spiritually grounded. You may be attracted to love others who need to be saved, but you could end up with people while confused, distant or dependent. If you keep a high level of drama in your life, it might be exhausting to you, but this might also be very important to you.

Neptune in the sixth house:

You easily gloss over the details of managing day to day affairs when Neptune is in the sixth house. Your personal philosophy is that life means more than just sticking to routines, making lists and managing bills. If you avoid or ignore these basic responsibilities, it can lead to confusion and chaos. You tend to give in to coworkers too easily, and you may not take credit for your own hard work. You may have big ideas regarding helping others, because you want to help others unconditionally. You need to draw some lines and boundaries so that you would not feel put down. There may be some health challenges that are hard to diagnosed, and you may be sensitive to drugs and allergies. Many of you may be compassionate to animals and pets.

Neptune in the seventh house:

You give more to partnerships then you take, especially marriage. You may also wear rose colored glasses when it comes to selecting a partner, and your perceptions in partnerships are not accurate. You need to take a step back consciously, so that you can see your partner and your relationship for what it is, rather for what you want it to be. Relationships with partners that need to be saved would attract you. Be careful of this, so that you would not end up with people who can confuse you, because they cannot comment, or may be overly sensitive and dependent. It is imperative that you set limits when it comes to choosing your partner for life. You can be accommodating with others, and you are a creative negotiator. You are talented in bringing out the good in another person, in particular, a partner.

Neptune in the eight house:

You long for spirituality. You may pay attention to your dreams and you are the type to analyze them. One of the strong role-playing in your life is sexual fantasies, and you yearn for a solo connection in a spiritual form. For some, there may be a feeling that their needs on this level are always out of reach. You might be a giver in bed, but then feel as though you give more than you get. If you find someone who is not giving as you are, you may left wanting, if Neptune is challenged, you may give more than you take with money, and you may be taken advantage of in a monetary level in partnership, if you adopt this attitude of what's mine is yours. And, you may lead yourself to deception or fraud. You have to take responsibility for your finances, and what is rightly yours. But, you can be sloppy with your finances.

Neptune in the ninth house:

You have a belief that anything is possible because you have faith in the universe. And, this faith can bring about positive circumstances. Do not depend too much on being saved. Make sure that your plans are taken off the ground, and do not neglect important details. If you keep your feet on the ground, the faith you have will carry you through. You need to recognize that you are in the driver seat, when it comes to your life. You have well developed spiritual beliefs. You are open and innovative to concepts and you are attracted to anything exotic. Some individuals may be easily led astray by religious or cults that do not serve them well. When seeking higher education, there may be chaos and you would need discipline in order to come complete it. You are excellent at promoting and marketing, because you can come up with creative methods of persuasion.

Neptune in the tenth house:

When it comes to current trends, business and what the public wants, you have a strong intuition about these issues. You would bring creativity, artistic, and vision to your career, which is good for working in the arts, and with media. If Neptune is afflicted, you can drift without a clear direction or lack to define your goals. It may hinder you from finding a calling in life, because of inner fears. This may contribute to the fact that you may not take responsibility for yourself. When you are in your chosen career, you may not get the recognition that you need. One your parents may have given you chaotic messages when you were a child, which would result in you finding it difficult to find a definite path in life. Others might take credit for your work. Do not incorporate other people's misconception about you.

Neptune in the eleventh house:

When Neptune is in the eleventh house, you may have "unfavorable conditions in friendship. Can be too gullible. Needs to have different night aims and goals in order to achieve success in life." (Hickey, 1992 p. 197) Your views are accepting and idealistic. Some of you would need to be more accommodating in your choice of friends, so that you would not be deceived or used. You may find it difficult and challenging to draw boundaries when it comes to how much you give of yourself, so that you can keep peace in your friendships. It might be difficult to get in touch with your feelings and deepest wishes of what will make you happy. You may attract or is attracted to artistic, sensitive, or unusual friends. You have much compassion and sympathy for the underdog or down trodden.

Neptune in the twelfth house:

You have unexceptional intuition and you are able to draw inner strength and faith, which might surprise others, because you are easy-going. You may be very sensitive, but you may not always be able to express your compassion directly. Do not deny the spiritual side of your nature, because you would not run the risk of discontent. If you do, you may feel vulnerable to normal changes in life. Your faith runs deep and it surfaces when you need it to be. It is also important that you believe in yourself. You may come into your spirituality later in life, which will help you to build a stronger identity. You do not like to feel as though you are confined. This is an excellent position for people in the health field, for example, doctors, nurses, etc.

Pluto in the houses:
Pluto in the first house:

You will know how to radiate intensity, and other peoples' first impressions of you are strong. You may intimidate others. You are the individual who is always protective of your privacy, but there is an intriguing and interesting thing about your presence. Few individuals are able to guess that you could be anything less than confident, yet you struggle with fears of being overpowered, rejected and minimized. When it comes to your instincts, it is determined, defensive, and intense. You do not accept things that are on the surface: because you do not accept the obvious. Instead, you look through situations, so that you can read the things that people want to hide. You do not view life as a battleground.

Pluto in the second house:

You have powerful instincts, when it comes to building your resources. It is hard for you to let go of things, because you attach sentimental values to your possessions. You hold onto them because you fear poverty, helplessness or wanting for anything. You feel a powerful need to control your money and the things that you possess. You will be driven to make money. When people take things from you without asking, it irritates you. This is not because you are stingy, but you have a strong sense of ownership. In order for you to learn the lessons of change, you may experience some forms of loss. You are a strategist and a great planner when it comes to your finances, and you know a good deal when you see one, and when you advise people in these areas, it is valuable.

Pluto in the third house:

You are not the one to accept what you hear or read. You have a very analytical and instinctive mind. When you express yourself in communication or in writing, you can be very persuasive. When you communicate, you do so with authority, strength and decisiveness. In order to learn, you need to observe, rather than ask than questions. You may be resilient when it comes to learning from others, because you prefer to be self-taught. You would choose your words wisely so that you can avoid others knowing that you know too much.

Pluto in the fourth house:

Due to early experiences, you may become secretive, and protective of yourself: because one of your parents may have been secretive, and you have learned this from him/her. Most of you may feel proud of your roots, yet you may feel guilt or shame, due to this. For some reason, one of your parents may have encouraged you to pursue the field of psychology. This parent may have also been very protective and tried to shield you from negative experiences. You have a fear for change. You may have had an experience in your earlier life that you are holding onto. You may have engrossed feelings of fears from one of your parents.

Pluto in the fifth house:

In romance, child rearing, creative arts, and passion, you have powerful creative impulses. You will take pride in whatever you produce. In your romance, you are intense, passionate, and deeply intimate. You want to get deeper into things, so that you can gain a better understanding. It is all or nothing for you in love. You need to own this attitude because you will meet it in someone else who is controlling. You are not lighthearted towards entertainment and recreation. However, fear may prevent you from getting involved in your creative endeavors.

Pluto in the sixth house:

You are definitely a hard worker and you are protective of the work that you do. However, you may become obsessed when it comes to finding answers to problems. You have an analytical mind. You become vibrant when you are presented with a problem that needs research. You can work tirelessly, because you can become obsessed: and you tend to become attached to what to do. You have the fear of being criticized. You are the one who needs to be your own boss. You may resent working for others, because they have control over your schedule. You have an interest in health and self- improvement.

Pluto in the seventh house:

There may be power struggle in close relationships, when Pluto is in the seventh house. There may be a combination of fear and desire may absorb you to one to one relationships. This may cause you to be resistant to partnerships, because you fear losing control over your own life. Be mindful because you may be drawn to people who are intense, possessive, obsessive and jealous. This is due to your ability to bring out the worst in others. Do not underestimate your role in this, and do not think that you are a victim. You will learn about your powers, which determines your outcome. Consequently, you tend to feel trapped in difficult relationships.

Pluto in the eight house:

You have on attraction to hidden things, and you may experience unusual events. You are a natural psychologist. It is easy for you to get to the heart of matters. Things that motivate you gain your interests. You love the mystical and mysterious things, also hypnosis. Your sexual experiences can be intense and complicated. You crave deep intimacy and

intense experiences, because you are fearful of deep intimacy. There may
be a power struggle with money. You would well in the healing
professions.

Pluto in the ninth house:

You are a self-opinionated person, and debates may turn into
arguments. You are intelligent and you are a persuasive individual. You
have strong opinions and they can be well reached. You have the ability to
back up your arguments. You may try to convert others to your beliefs,
which can make you obsessive. However, you may become suspicious of
new ideas until you have proven them yourself. You literary hate
hypocrisy. There is a reason that you may be considered deep, and you are
the type to come up with unique ideas. You have a deep sense of
adventure. You are an inspiring speaker, teacher, and lecturer. You love to
travel and make new connections.

Pluto in the tenth house:

Your sense of destiny is powerful. However, you can have a well
driven attitude in the way you pursue your careers. This may even attract
admirers and opponents. There is a radical side to you and you want to
change the world. You are a very powerful force for healing and making
changes in the world, based on your astrological position. The changes
will begin with you, especially when you feel ambitious, and you strive for
more. Transformation brings spiritual aspiration, especially in goal
oriented areas of your life. You desire a sense of power. As you gain this
power, your presence and strength may attract power struggle with others.
You will rub shoulders with movers and shakers, because that is where
you belong. Bury your resentments. You will heal others because of their
wounds, which is the keys to liberate others.

Pluto in the eleventh house:

You may have a deep hatred for organization clubs of any kind,
and if you get involved in them: it is for your own personal growth. Your
circumstances may compel you to change. You may want to follow other
people's dreams. You must weigh all your inner voices, so that you can
understand what they are saying to you. There may also be power
struggles within your social circle. Women do not want to sit on the
sidelines, because they love to do things effectively. Be careful not to fall

under the influence of others. You can be an influential leader, once you have been awakened to your own desires.

Pluto in the twelfth house:

You love secrets and mysterious things, and you will psychoanalyze your dreams, so that you can uncover the secrets. You are intuitive and your subconscious energies will bring transformation that was influenced by your previous life. Deaths that you have dealt with could have caused the doubts that you harbor about your abilities. It is vital that you use your private time to pay attention to your knowledge. Use your confidence to replace any doubts and fears. It is also important to have a quiet time by yourself. You may also want to hold on to your feelings. There is a possibility that you may have problems with addiction and depression. Also, you may also have emotional problems about ghosts of the past. However, when you conquer your demons, you will be able to help others.

Triplicities:

Triplicities have to do with signs belonging to the same element. However, the signs are 120° apart, which is formed as an angle. The angle is called a trine. These connections are free-flowing: making the signs in each element comfortable and compatible with each other. The names of the triplicities are fire, air, earth, and water. The trine or triad represents the origin or time that the soul enters the body at birth, the form of life and the soul returns to its parent at death. This virtually represents completion or a complete cycle. Also, this can be compared to the holy Trinity: meaning three in one and one in three. In each triplicity, there is a planetary ruler; a day ruler and a night ruler.

Air	Libra, Aquarius, Gemini	Sanguine	Wet, becoming Hot
Fire	Aries, Leo, Sagittarius	Choleric	Hot, becoming Dry
Earth	Capricorn, Taurus, Virgo	Melancholic	Dry, becoming cold
Water	Cancer, Scorpio, Pisces	Phlegmatic	Cold, becoming wet

Lehman, 1996, p. 43

Fire:

The fire signs Aries, Leo, and Sagittarius. Their day ruler is the Sun; night ruler is Jupiter and the participating ruler is saturated. These signs normally hunt for things that light them up. There is a burst of energy and enthusiasm. Individuals with his sign (fire) can flare up when they are inspired, and they are passionate about life. They are very intuitive and they use their faith and inner feelings to guide them. "The element fire refers to a universe of radiant energy, an energy which is excitable, enthusiastic, and which through its light brings color to the world. This element has been correlated with the dynamic core of psychic energy. (Arroyo, 1975 p. 95)

Air:

Furthermore, air represents energy of life. The planets in air signs use their mind and make sense of things and their lives. And at times, individuals tend to appear detached from others. It is easy to talk their way through things and analyze them carefully. Flexibility is associated with air signs, and they can experience life through many facets. People with air signs are excellent communicators and they can make great storytellers, and journalists, and they would be able to interpret things easily. "The air realm is the world of archetypal ideas behind the veil of the physical world, the cosmic energy actualize into specific patterns of thought. It is associated with geometric lines of force functioning through the mind that energy which shapes the patterns of things to come." (Arroyo, 1975, p. 96)

Earth:

This element can be considered a less action oriented. It is considered to be more grounded than the other elements, and an individual will see no reason to be skipping around like a hummingbird, expending all that energy. Individuals with this element in their sign tend to be very dependable about their goals. They tend to be consistent, which is part of their nature. However, this person is most likely to fall into bad habits, and he or she may have attributes of creativity in music and arts, which is a typical manifestation of this element. Routine and structure is something that they find comfort in, during their daily activities, and they are most likely to see the broad picture of reality: before taking action.

Water:

There is an in-depth creativity about this element, and it is most comfortable when dealing with emotions and spirituality. People with this grand trine experience life with emotional intensity, and they react to life's events on the sub conscious level. This fuels their choices, instead of thinking about them and their intuition is usually correct. Furthermore, their feeling may drain them on a spiritual and psychological level, but they should not become too oversensitive because it can be a problem.

The triplicities are called the grind trine, and are considered to be the purest expression of the elements. There are positive aspects of the signs, and each aspect has its high and lows, and can be better or worse in many circumstances. The trine's tendency is to create harmony and flow of energy between the planets. It reveals where someone's planets might be or it may indicate whether the individual is lazy. Also, it shows if the individual will be an active participant or just tagging along. "The trine emphasizes expression that is innately creative, warming, and positive sense of self, contentment, internal confidence, and general well-being." (Tierney, 183, p. 27)

The guardruplicities are also referred to as molds and they ruled different values: and of course, they have characteristics of their own. They are also referred to as the grand cross or grand square because there are four signs, planets, houses and all areas of life that connected together. The mode or quality is: cardinal, fixed, and mutable, and they form four squares and two oppositions. Each mode has its own expression and interpretation, which is unique. They motivate action. Tension may develop over time, and cause us to reduce some of it when the time comes. They can either be constructive or destructive. The important thing is to develop a balance between the two oppositions.

Cardinal:

With the Cardinal signs, people focused on the self and their identity, and actions that surround them. The individual may have the ability to impulsively express the self. For some, there is an emotional identity that needs to be nurtured, and for others: there is and intellectual identity that is connected to tangible manifestation, a need to be recognized for one's own identity. The four cardinal planets are pushing in order to express the different facets of the self, but each of the planets

110

operates from a different level of perspective. This is a mode of action, and individuals in this mode are great initiators, but they need to maintain a sense of focus, at all times.

Fixed:

Signs that are fixed show that an individual focuses on his/her self-worth, but it is directed on whether or not the individual has the ability to recognize the worth of the self. Some people tend to have self-mastery, creativity and the spirit of vulnerability, trust, humanity, and brotherhood. These individuals are fixed in their ways, and are not always ready to move, take action, or make efforts to implement change. This is due to the fact that that they do not like to be pressured to make changes. There is great resistance with fixed signs, especially when it comes to maintaining homeostasis and balance. But, when individuals take action it can be difficult to stop their momentum, until they have achieved their goals. The challenge is: individuals find it difficult to be flexible.

Mutable:

These signs are more focused on healing and reasoning. A great amount of that focus is directed on the ability to integrate thoughts and feelings, how to organize concepts, use diversity and wisdom, or show compassion and the spirit. With mutable sign, it can be easy to be scattered when under pressure. On the downside, it may be difficult for mutable signs to guide their thoughts because they are always thinking. The most important thing is: individuals need to learn how to gain a sense of balance and coordination. This should be a main goal. The individual will gain the most when they learn how to maintain a sense of consistency while juggling their activities. The productivity of the mutual sign is always to remain flexible and adaptable, and avoid any obstacle that is placed in its path.

Equinox:

The equinox is the point of the earth's annual orbit around the sun, where the indication of the right angles of the line that is drawn between the Earth and the sun. This all depends on the length of the day and night, and how they are equal all over the earth. This takes place at two points, which is called the Vernal Equinox. However, this occurs when Earth passes on March 21st when it enters Aries, and on September 22nd when it enters Libra. The equinox can be commonly demarcated at the moment

111

when the sun reaches the point where the plane of the ecliptic intersects with the plane of the equator.

Solstice:

This is an astronomical event that takes place twice per year, when the sun's position in the sky reaches its northern most and southernmost extremes. The sun stands still in declination and the apparent movement of the Sun's path in the north or south comes to a stop. The solstice is connected to seasons, and can be viewed as the beginning or ending of a season, and it may fall in the middle in some cultures. The solstice can also be referred to as "sun standing". However, the day before and after the solstice declination speed is less than the 30 arc seconds per day. The solstice is formed because the Earth's axis is tilted and forms a perpendicular to the plane, and it gives the four seasons their meaning. Also, when it begins, it is normally the longest day of the year marking the beginning of summer, and the beginning of winter, which is the shortest day of the year.

Masculine and feminine groupings of the signs:

Evidently, the polarities in the signs have an association of masculine and feminine, which is a representative of Yin and Yang. This is the primary division of the chart. They are also known as negative and positive, introverted and extroverted, and odd and even. The principal division is the basis of dual physical universe. Furthermore, there are six masculine and six feminine signs. Masculine signs: Aries, Gemini, Leo, Libra, Sagittarius and Aquarius. Feminine signs: Taurus, Cancer, Virgo, Scorpio, Capricorn, and Pisces. When a planet is in its home sign, the masculine and feminine is pure and will remain balanced, and there is little or no inclination towards what may call sexuality.

In fact, the signs, elements, or gender may lose its balance when the planet leaves the home sign. Furthermore, planets blend in nature and forces when they are in the same elements, genders, signs, or if they are in closed aspect by degree. Basically, the most common form of blending occurs went two planets are in the same gender. However, planets in the same elements blend more; also planets in the same sign of blending most of all, and they help and reinforce each other. This: of course, helps them to maintain a perfect male and female equilibrium. Individuals with this in

their charts tend to be more content with themselves. Mercury in Taurus
tends to be sensual; naturally an individual can go to the extreme.

Aspects and their meaning:

"An aspect is the angular relationship between two points in the
360° of the zodiac. All the planets in a horoscope are located in the zodiac,
and the angle between any two planets, given in degrees is called and
aspect." (Pelletier, 1974 xix) Furthermore, the interactions between the
planets are considered aspects; which measures the ecliptic plane.
However, only certain relationships are considered to be aspects with a
certain amount of qualities. It is important to pay close attention to the
number of degrees. To better understand the aspects, one must first
understand that the planets have an influence on man's behavior, and the
environment as well.

Furthermore, interpreting aspects in the chart is very crucial.
According to Tierney (1983) "aspects weave powerful and purposeful
energy patterns. Connecting the many parts of the chart. They trace out a
highly complex, unduplicated montage of force-fields designed for
promoting the individualization of each developing human psyche." (p. 1)
It helps to show how motivated someone is, and can expose any hidden
things in someone's life. The nature of the aspect is also revealed and
reflected in the corresponding house.

Conjunction:

The planets that form the conjunction produced energies that unite
with each other. They blend and act together. The closer they are, the more
combined their energies are. These planets do not stand alone, and they
may have a difficult time acknowledging each other being distinct from
each other. Conjunctions are also called blind spots. "Since the
conjunction aspect is 0°, it technically makes no arc. Because of this, it
does not fall into the category of either a standard waxing or waning
aspect. If anything, the conjunction becomes an aspect partly shared by
both hemicycles." (Tierney, 1983 p. 6) In fact, when the degrees are exact,
it is difficult to differentiate the vibration of either one.

As an example, if someone has a Sun-Mercury conjunction, he or
she would be able to identify and rationalize with their mind. That the
individual will know how to use the mind to organize his or her thoughts,
and knows how to identify with the thoughts and opinions. An individual

113

who do not have this aspect may find it easier to accept that he or she have thoughts, ideas, and opinions. Whatever they are thinking are only a part of the whole person, and does not reflect the whole person. Conjunctions have an effect on one's personal identity. Consequently, people who have charts that are dominated by conjunctions are very self driven and motivated individuals. In fact, they do not look outside of the self for self-definition or for validation, but they are confident in who they are and what they stand for.

They do not need a mirror to view themselves, but they know who they are and what they stand for. Conjunctions are easier to spot in the chart, and they give clues on how it affects the individual. However, planets that are in conjunct tend to be difficult to interpret, because of the energies involved. This is the most powerful aspect possible, since there is more than one planet involved. "A conjunction produces a more concentrated energy and force so that the planets involved are more easily expressed. It inclines the person to assert the blended qualities of the two planets with little regard for the effect this has on other people." (Pelletier, 1974 p. 17) The dynamics of the planets express creativity for the individual, and he or she displays a great amount of enthusiasm to move past any obstacles that are in the way. In fact, the individual can be very competitive, and would be willing to face challenges that come up. The individual may not favor being criticized and will show discomfort when this happens.

Semi Sextile:

This aspect offer support and confirm information that is already in the chart. "The rule is simple: two planets are considered to be in their waxing or lower aspect phase when the faster planet is approaching the opposition point of this lower planet according to the natural sequence of signs. Usually in the chart, the quick planet would always be found located on the right hand (dexter)" (Tierney, 1983 p. 10) When two planets are in their waning it means the faster planet will separate from the slower planet which is heading towards reconjuncting with a planet. The planet that is moving faster would occupy the lower half of the cycle. However, the semi sextile has a suppressive nature and it corresponds with both water and fire signs.

They build the potential of life naturally. In this phase, the attraction of resources is dealt with, which processes a need for

114

development. When the semi sextile is in an earth sign, the individual would be productive, especially when it comes to material things and he or she is self-sustaining, and would be able to manifest. Consequently, the semi sextile cannot produce enough force to kindle us so that we can use any resources in our daily interactions. It is easy for you to gravitate towards any environments that are balanced. When it is in Mercury, you will appreciate how the human mind has a clear and precise understanding of nature. It is easy for you to support educational standards, especially among young children. "This aspect enables us to draw from the hidden facets of our inner self. Soul goods may manifest as creative imagination, visualize power, psychic impressionability, and mystical experience." (Tierney, 1983 p. 13 &14)

Semi Square:

In the semi-square planets are 45° apart of each other. The circle is divided by eight square aspects, which shows energy that is blocked between two planets in your chart. It shows that the events that are taking place are external, and you will be forced to face and address any difficulties that you need to deal with. However, the semi-square can lead you to accomplish and achieve things that are tangible. Individuals with this aspect develop great persistence, and would have productive results in their efforts to conquer any difficult situations. You are a natural initiator and would be the first to start things.

You may also develop attitudes that will keep you inadaptable and resistant to make changes. You possess a degree of strength and persistence, and when your mind is made up, it is hard to change it. The semi-square is also known as an irritant aspect. Furthermore, "the Gemini factor also is teaching us to remain mentally adaptable concerning our attitudes towards social consciousness." (Tierney, 1983 p.7) But, for individuals who are not inspired, there is no social objectives, they may appear to be hateful and may shun others, through their cranky behavior.

Sextile:

When two planets are 60° apart, they are considered to be sextile, because the circle is divided by six. There is a relation to the major trine. There are always three sides in between what separates the sextile. It usually points to the talents that you appreciate in yourself. Sextiles are more communicative and shows strong relationship with each other, and how their energies can be directed. It is also called the aspect of opportunity, pleasure, enjoyment, and intellectual visualization. Dancers and musicians would link with this sextile because it is linked with rhythm and repetition. Also, sextile is known as the aspect of harmony. "The sextile aspect combines the dynamics of planets. The signs occupied by the planets involved congenial whether they are positive or negative. The sextile aspect compels the planets influences to function mainly in the intellectual world of ideas." (Pelletier, 1974 p. 71)

However, it shows how a person organizes his or her thoughts, and what subjects are of great interest to them. This individual is very sharp, and knows how to communicate effectively, and would know how to gather the information. People under the sign of Gemini will know how to understand multifaceted subjects and knows how to interpret them intelligently for others to understand. Also, it is related to creativity, and act as a medium of expression. You will be able to adapt to new incoming information. People with this quantity aspect would love to have a broader connection of contacts and this will help to enrich their life.

Square:

The square is the cusp of cancer. Energies are drawn inward. There is an imbalance that needs to be addressed because the harmony is disrupted. This aspect shows a need to rewrite and achieve something tangible. It also shows that something is not finished or it may be out of balance. The person with planets that are squared shows an area in his or her life that needs to be worked on, in order to find peace and harmony. Consequently, there may be a conflict around the energies that are expressed by the planets. This is what drives people forward, so that they can accomplish their goals, but there may also be an underlying intention, which makes it hard to be around them. Moreover, these people love change and they will change the world around them in the process.

The pressure of the square is further highlighted and by the fact that when planets are three signs apart, they are sitting in signs of completely different elements. Furthermore, when the signs are not compatible, they would be connected and would have to find a way to be reconciled with each other. The square is the driving force in someone's life, and they need to be resolved and accepted. "The initial effect of this square is to cause frustration when the psychological factors corresponding to either of the planets are involved. Some adjustments

116

must be made before one can use the energies positively. This aspect shows that there are lessons to be learned." (Pelletier, 1974 p. 125) The lessons that you have learned, ultimately will be a test, and when you pass the test, your character would be built. You will, across as being perfect to others. All the greatest tests in life come through the square aspects, and you will gain mastery over the unconscious.

Sesqi Square:

When two planets are 135° apart, they are known as sesqui square. The links between the planets are different and the attributes to the psyche can also be proven to be difficult, as well. Due to this difficulty, it can shoot the individual to greater heights with his or her efforts to achieve balance and harmony, and with this creativity: the individual will find it quite easy to create tangible results, even though the path may not be easy. "The individual is pressured to apply more self-control and emotional voice if he is to effectively channel this aspect, since here he tends to react irrationally or act immoderately at the expense of others." (Tierney, 1983 p. 32) In this case, the individual is putting his needs above that of others, but his extreme behavior can lead towards conflicts in his or her experience.

Furthermore, the individual would react to minor struggles in a dynamic manner, which of course will throw the situations out of balance and out of proportion. And in the end, will create anger and resentment. The lower sesqui square correlates with the fifth house and the Sun, and it represents the rude side of the individual, which is powered by the ego. You tend to be an attention seeking individual, which is done in a childish manner; and in the end, you can alienate others. When you receive criticism, you become very defensive. You have a drive to think that everything pertaining to you are important, and this can cause you to behave in a dominating manner, and others would take you as being rude.

Quincunx:

This aspect is in an even division of the 360 circle. It also produces an elegant number, which is the essence of this aspect, and it is a difficult one. However, the two planets that involves cannot see or communicate with each other, because they are not straight in front of each other, because they are slightly tilted. But, in some way: they are related to each other, and they are five signs away from each other. The elements and

117

modes are not the same. It is not an easy aspect to deal with, because actions have been simultaneously, which makes it difficult to see a connection between the two elements. Once there is an understanding between the planets, the hidden gift that is connected to this aspect can be seen. This gives true meaning to the phrase "opposites attract". The planets that are involved in the Quincunx will keep the other planets in check because they hold the key that the other planets do not have.

Most importantly, the signs do not confront each other, because they do not see each other. The Quincunx will describe stress that shows up in your chart, because there is always a conflict. In fact, if the Quincunx associates itself with any health problems, they would not be life threatening. "The Quincunx can be viewed more aptly as a "nagging" problem, operating over an extended period of time. It lacks the intensity and strength of impact required to bring its tension to our surface consciousness until almost in a faithful manner, circumstances develop forcing us to give it our utmost attention." (Tierney, 1983 p. 36) When this irritating problem manifests in the individual's life, he or she will have to take action to resolve them.

Opposition:

When two planets are opposite each other they are considered to be opposition, and they are 180° apart from each other. The two should act as one, so there will be no disharmony or opposing ideas. The analogy of the opposition is like to the Yin and Yang, which are the two primary forces. Also, the aspects of creating man and woman, night and day, up and down, left and right, and right and wrong is likened to the opposition. This has a lot to do with polarity. This division is fundamental and necessary to creation. In order to have freedom of choice, separation, and things to achieve, there must be an opposition. This way, you can confront and make the necessary changes. The duality in the opposition is a dynamic that animates creation.

"The opposition resolves the psychological misalignment produced by the two planets involved. Initially the aspects causes alienation in relationships, because one is not able to resolve the raging conflict and controversy set up by the planets." (Pelletier, 1974 p.277) In essence, when the planets are in a position, they will reflect the qualities of each other, but there may be a tension because they do not agree, as they are coming from both sides. Consequently, they are vital to each other, so that

118

they would reach an understanding and create balance. Also, it represents fundamental forces in the individual's psyche, if they are in need of reconciliation. This will cause the individual to see the things that need to be changed in the other person: because it is difficult to see it in himself or herself.

As an illustration, if someone has an opposition between the Moon and Mars, he or she would have both forces on the inside of them. And, the person will have a desire to powerfully express his or her emotions. With the Moon in opposition, you may feel emotional, but not powerful because you are attracted to powerful people. This is due to the fact that you will resonate this with your unexpressive feelings. This will show you what is on the inside of you. In fact, once you acknowledge the power that is on the inside of you, you will understand that you do not need to seek it from the outside world. With opposition in your chart, you will learn through your relationships, and you will learn what is on the inside of you. However, you will find yourself trying to make some important changes. You will also build barriers to protect your vulnerability and insecurities.

Furthermore, if there is any uneasiness in the opposition, the aspect of influence will show up and will be projected in other people. You may feel embarrassed about the attitudes that are in other people, because they are on the inside of you. This shows how the opposition is the easiest to resolve the conflicts, in all of the aspects. Whatever problems are present, will be easy to work out, because the opportunity would present itself. You will become more conscious of yourself and of the things that would help you to move on. When you live out all sides, and acknowledge the things that need to be changed: you will become whole. Air and fire signs are compatible with each other. Opposition brings forth awareness, and it will bring forth things to our attention. "When well integrated, the planets enhance each other's function pulling together for the benefit of the greater whole." (Tierney, 1983 p. 39)

The uncommon aspects:
The Qunitile:

This aspect is angled at 72° and it is linked with a distinct tendency to be one pointed, and it is forcefully driven in a focused field of activity. It divides the circle with harmony. "The quintile represents the fifth Harmonic. The quintile family includes multiplies such as a semi-quintile

(30°), the sesqui-quintile (108°), and the bi-quintile (144°). (Tierney, 1983 p. 46) It is protuberant in the charts of victims and criminals of any violent act, or individuals who dictate. This is when it is in its negative expression. However, when it is in its positive expression, it will be distinctive in the chart of artists and writers. Also, it is related with the mysteries and hermetic magic. This is the symbol of the contender's creative soul.

Bi Quintile:

At one under 44° position in the chart, lies the bi-quintile. It also plays a part in the harmonic theory that will continue to divide the circle in five of 18°. This is one of the minor aspects. It only applies to the Sun, Mercury, and Sun Venus aspects because of the proximity of the Sun to Mercury and Venus. This aspect will say something about your personal style and about your creative work, as well. There is a unique relationship between the mind and the quintiles, and it gives form to how we process information, either orally or through written form. Also, how we describe the way in which we communicate. People who formulate and link things together have the quintile very predominant in their chart. It also shows the kind of art you are drawn to, and if you have the power to dominate. Furthermore, the quintiles also describes the potential and abilities, which are normally considered to be exceptional or gifted, and the abilities that are not developed.

Septile:

The septile is the seventh harmonic aspect, which is one seventh of the 360° circle. As an illustration, if Neptune septile Pluto appears in your natal chart, then your destiny is to fulfill the midwife of the spirit, and you want to change and convert the deepest parts of your being. And, this is felt as a divine importance in your life, and regardless to any sacrifice you would not waver from your path. One of your realizations is that you think that you are meant to share the fruits all the efforts to assist others. Furthermore, you have a great imagination, insight and understand and you have reverence for the cycles of life. The careers that you will gravitate to are: spiritual, surgeon, and the field of psychology.

"The set time aspect corresponds with the number seven and the 7th harmonic. Throughout the ages, the number seven has been associated with sacred, holy matters as any student well-versed in religious symbolism knows. Neurology change interprets seven as a very occult number." (Tierney, 1983 p. 50) Anything to do with the knowledge that you have acquired for yourself is linked with the septile. You yearn for the meaning of wisdom, and how you can use it to your disposal. The numbers what urges you to heavily investigate the deeper essence of your reality. The number seven has to do with meditation, isolation and contemplation. It also shows that the individual can get to a place of solitude. Also, it is a symbol of God resting on the seventh day after doing His work; therefore, it is a representation of being remote and aloof.

Novile:

The novile is a minor aspect, which lies between two planets that measure 40°. It is also the ninth harmonic of the angle in your chart. The interesting thing is when two points are novile; it forms a geometric position on Earth to show that two bodies appear to be 1/9 of the zodiac. The number nine is a perfect square, and it's symbolism represents idealism: which can be both spiritual and material. Also, it specifies and spiritual growth, through your source of responsibility, when it is activated. It is 1/3 of the trine and this makes it both harmonious and lucky. In order for the two points to be novile, they must not be in the same elements or quality, and they may or may not be in the same gender; the interesting thing is: any incompatible sign combines in absolute harmony.

It also represents selflessness and universal understanding. Some of the ways that it expresses itself is through showing compassion. You will be a very forgiving, tolerant, and benevolent individual, and you are willing to sacrifice yourself for the healing of humanity. Because the number nine represents the novile, it shows completion and fulfillment. On the other hand, it also represents some unfinished business, because it is the last of phase of the cycle. The novile loves to be in the back ground and does not like to be seen. "Esoterically, number nine has a special evolutionary influence. "To quote Heline the strange phenomenon of nine in its power (suggests that) the matter by what number it is multiplied... It eternally reproduces itself." (Tierney, 1983 p. 54)

Dissociate aspects:
Dissociate conjunction:

This involves signs that are semi-sextile of each other, and they do not unite or focus their energies. The signs are different and their motivations have no similarity. Of course, they do not combine as easily, if the planets have conflict in this position. You may not feel as motivated to affirm yourself in any direct and impulsive manner. You will have the tendency to act with less force, and you may feel a bit awkward and a bit uneasy about expressing yourself, even if you want to. Therefore, you will evaluate your actions before moving on your instincts: before you get involved in an activity. It is easy to draw from your inner feelings. For example, you will be able to bring things into the material world.

Dissociate semi sextile:

"The out-of-sign semi-sextile involves the underlying influence of the conjunction or sextile. When the two planets of the dissociate semi-sextile are both in the same sign, there could be a psychological reluctance." (Tierney, 1983 p. 58) When you are in your independent world, you can move towards your nurturing experiences which would foster the growth of your inner resources. Because this aspect is in direct, the influence that it has is less noticeable. The perspective is even more dormant. When you establish a better sense of identity and self-image, you will be motivated to work with your inner resources. It is easy to fuel the drive to push towards manifestation. The individual is naturally curious about everything, and wants to know how things are applied. And, you would find an intelligent and inventive way to attract the resources that you need.

Dissociate sextile:

There are underlying influences with this aspect that proposes a lap of facility distinctive of the standard sextile. "The dissociate sextile involving signs that semi-sextile one another is that the less bother some of the two. Although the individual has no trouble attracting constructive opportunities, he may feel less stimulated by them and thus may pass them up." (Tierney, 1983, p. 59) The inactiveness of this dissociate sextile may discourage you from open self-expression, because there is an inner resistance when it comes to learning new things. You will have to make a conscious effort to become more malleable and adaptable in your attitude, if you are to fully benefit from the experiences that you attract. You may find that you may benefit from things slowly, but they would be valued and appreciated.

Dissociate square:

As an individual with this in your chart, you will attract challenging situations that may force you to confront the matters head on. But, this may cause you to lack stamina and determination to deal with any demanding situation. However, the standard squares are more powerful because the signs that are involved will challenge each other's expression. When this dissociate Square is managed properly, it could prove to be most stimulating, and you will identify any inner conflicts. This way: any concrete patterns would be broken. On the other hand, the well-managed dissociate Square indicates that an individual's sense of harmony will allow him to accept challenges with faith and confidence. It does not matter how difficult things get, but you will believe that they will work out for the better. You will have to cultivate your self-discipline so that you can resist any temptation.

Dissociate trine:

With this out of sign trine, it can be found in the quincunx or square one another. This represents any underlying influences, which will trigger any psychological disharmony and uneasiness that is embedded within the mind of the individual. However, if this dissociate trine is in signs that a quincunx off each other, you would not be able to adjust psychologically to the benefits that you attract. You will become out of focus on your inner strength: which results in you being dissatisfied with the outcome of their daily activities. When this happens, you would not be able to relax and enjoy the benefit what a trine offers. However, you may find yourself making adjustments in areas that you really do not require any adjustments. With this trine, there is a lack of confidence on your part which results in becoming insecure.

Dissociate quincunx:

"The out-of-sign quincunx can occur in signs that either trine or oppose each other. The orb must be kept small (3° or less). When the dissociate quincunx operates through thru signs, the individual inwardly may have a positive or optimistic attitudes." (Tierney, 1983 p. 83) This individual will show an energetic burst of interest in reorganizing the parts of himself or herself that hinders them from functioning at the optimal level. You have a strong intuition and you would be able to visualize in your mind the things that you want to change. By doing this, you will come to the strong psychological willingness to improve yourself in a

123

more meaningful way; and you will be able to enjoy the changes that were made. Consequently, this can be harmful to some extent: because you may add to the ongoing problem.

Dissociate opposition

This dissociate opposition involves signs that are naturally quincunx each other. In this position, the individual can make the necessary corrections and adjustments concerning his or her relationships. Oppositions normally give you the opportunity to view things on both sides of any situation making the necessary changes: which only occurs in the normal opposition. But, with the dissociate opposition; an individual may not be willing to observe the situation in a correct and accurate manner. This is a blind spot and the individual may become irritated by this. In this aspect, one may become uncertain: which would cause anxiety in the way he handles his relationships, and the challenges that they produce. Even though external conflicts may be less ostensible your actual union, the inner conflicts are fitting to be less critical

Qualities, elements, and signs in aspects:
The cardinal cross:

The cardinal cross tends to create conflicts which rotates mainly around the essentials of any personal family life. How you can go directly for what you want for yourself, and also meet the needs of your partner and partnerships. With all of this going on in your life you are still interested in carving a place in society for yourself, in the form of the career, but, you will make time for emotional, domestic, and your family life. It would also show whether or not you want to be a parent. When people have the cardinal aspects in their chart, they usually make attempts to deal with any conflicts, when confronted with them. Because of this strategy, they know how to detach themselves from problems: because they tackled them head on, but they do it without any sagacity and without thinking about it.

The cardinal oppositions:
Aries-Libra:

This represents the other individual that you consider yourself opposing then (I versus you). The individual is into the things that please himself or herself, but is considering what the other person desires, and how things can work out. Meaning: you want to give and take, so that you can play the game of life fairly. You deserve to maintain your own individuality and your position, yet you want to cooperate, so you can view things from your own perspective, other than your own. You may find yourself being concerned about relationships, especially the one to one relationships. With both signs being associated with war: when they combine, Aries takes the responsibility for combat and Libra is all about fairness and justice. There are many of you who will fight for what you value the most.

Cancer-Capricorn:

Flexibility versus inflexibility, family versus occupation, public life versus private life. These combinations tends to be traditional which gives you the opportunity to be responsible and discipline. You take care of your family and can hold a powerful place in society, and you have a great respect for the past and also for your roots. With Cancer, individuals tend to be sensitive and nurturing, and with Capricorn: they are more aware of the need for family, and societal boundaries, limitations and laws. Cancer may say "I love you because you are mine", and Capricorn says "I love you if you stay within the limits". When they are correctly shared, they can be ideal parents, because this opposition views with parenting. Ideally, Cancer is the substantial and significant one in the home, especially with family. Capricorn represents society as a whole and on the state, also have a political view point.

Aries-Cancer:

This combination can often get aroused whenever the family seems to be under threat about personal matters. Major conflicts may arise between the signs because Aries principle is independent and self orienting. However, Cancer is dependent and family oriented. This person tends to be a home body. In all essence, there may be some conflict need to strike out and pulled on the family and the past. Due to some type of tension, the individual may feel very frustrated. This is a good combination for individuals who are trying to get away from the past. Aries-Cancer can be found advocating causes for or against issues that interest the individual. In fact, this is an ideal combination to show that the individual crusades on behalf of his or her family.

Aries-Capricorn:

People with this Cardinal square in their chart is very ambitious and go getting. They have the apt of being entrepreneurs, because of their drive and ability to initiate. The desired to get to the top may result in the individual stepping on some people: not caring whether or not he or she use fairness or foul play to get there. If you have the desire to achieve something too quickly, it may cause you to get frustrated and dissatisfied with the rules and restrictions enforced by the outer world. You would be led to make the effort for you to resist authority. People who come up against the government normally have this aspect in their chart; this is an individual who struggle to get to the top of the ladder in society. Also, you will set goals that may seem unreachable to others.

Cancer-Libra:

There is a strong concern with partnership, family and home issues, when these two signs are in the chart. The individual may enter into a relationship to build a family life. The attention and demands on the family may be challenging, because you want one to one interaction with another individual. With cancer, there is a strong need for security and Libra wants someone who will reflect, do and, share things with. Stress on those two signs can be evident in someone's chart, and it may be difficult for the individual to stand on his or her own two feet, so that you can cope on your own. This is a flexible and yielding combination, and you are easily persuaded on most things. In relationships, there may be some conflicts because Libra wants for equality is a discrepancy with the Cancerian tendency in relationship to nurture or be nurtured.

Libra-Capricorn:

With these two signs in the chart, people may come across as being smooth. They have the tendency to be very civil, with a calm collective attitude. This is an ideal combination for anyone in the public. You care deeply about what others think, and you are sensitive to external opinion. You have a strong need to be respected. When most people enter into partnerships, it is for prestigious reasons. There may be a challenge to balance the attention between your relationships and your career. While Capricorn concerns itself with discipline and order, Libra focuses on fairness and equality. Libra is indecisive while Capricorn is authoritative, but there is a conflict between these two signs and it is impossible to draw an authoritarian line between both, on certain issues. Both signs are associated with the law.

The fixed cross:
The fixed oppositions:
Taurus-Scorpio:

Tranquility versus emotional storms, the builder versus the eco-warrior. These two signs are apprehensive with attachment and desire, ranging from sex and money. When this polarity is stressed on the natal chart, the feelings of rage, jealousy, and envy are expected and they must be confronted. This happens when there are one or more oppositions in the chart. These two signs are concerned with completing deep psychic contact with others, and with one's own soul. Because Taurus is fixed Earth, it is more rooted in the physical and security, and in the gathering of possessions. Taurus is also concerned with sex for essential enjoyment of the senses.

Leo-Aquarius:

The self versus the group, individual differences versus John public, the dictator versus the egalitarian, the sculptor to versus the researcher, slavery versus freedom. Aquarius will speak on being the Democratic member of a group, while Leo pursues to lead and wants to be the ruler of everything that it governs. With Leo, nothing happens without an audience. When people have this polarity in their chart, they tend to be very proud, fixed and set in their ways, and being different from the crowd. The way they cope with the dictator/freedom of speech dilemma is by gaining a position of individuality which of course, encourages Aquarius morals of equal opportunities. They are well known for the own brand of originality. It can be possible that this polarity is more concerned with love and friendship.

The fixed squares:
Taurus-Leo:

These signs are a solid and reliable combination, but they are inclined to be stubborn and rigid. There is also pride found in this pair, and they have and appreciation for the good life. The individual will have a taste for good food and wine, and desires to have physical, comfort especially luxurious items. There may also be health problems due to overconsumption of rich foods, but if the individual gets involved with projects that require some type of physical activity: this problem can be obsolete. People hope and wish for meaningful emotional and sexual relationship, as well and it can lead to overindulgence. When dealing in business and financial awareness along with the power of money, this pair is ideal. Taurus is steady and proceeds with caution, while Leo is the risk taker. Together, they are creative.

Taurus-Aquarius:

Taurus is a sign that is concerned with individualism, attachment and tradition and in building a physically secure existence. But, on the other hand, Aquarius is strange and detached and has a major concern with friendship and group life. The conflict between the two signs are easy to detect, but people with this square can gain a solid foundation from Taurus and its stability. However, people are often concerned with the physical and material problems of society, when this square is in their chart. They are possessive of their freedom, but they may also concern themselves with everybody else enjoying the same benefits. People with this square in their charts are often interested in living the simple life, and they love to enjoy nature and the outdoor life. They also love to share information.

Leo-Scorpio:

People with this combination are considered to be warm and passionate, but there is pride and joy along with some streak of stubbornness, as part of their character. This duo loves power and status: which is important to the individual. The combination will allow people to work with money very easily; Scorpio works with other people's money and Leo works with the bank. Individuals will do well working as bank managers, financial officers, loan and mortgage consultants and chief financial officers. There is a conflict with this combination, because Leo loves to be seen, while Scorpio wants things to remain quiet and private. People with this combination in their chart normally have a flair for drama, and would make excellent actors and actresses. However, they may harbor ill feelings and may not be the first to forgive.

Scorpio-Aquarius:

Because Scorpio loves to keep everything private, there is a conflict with this combination. Aquarius is outgoing friendly and honest and wants to share their feelings. For the individual to overcome this conflict, he or she would do things in and unconventional manner, so that individuality will be dominant in the daily routine. Psychology is an interest to both signs, but from different perspectives, and group therapy would be a part of their regimen. They are creative in the ideas and their feelings run deep, which may peek someone's interest in something, but only for a brief moment. However, the person may be restless and appears to be cold towards others, but to the individual who wants to transform the world, it is ideal with in this chart. You would not back down from anything or anyone. You may be antisocial, because you are not concerned with social particulars.

Mutable cross:
The mutable oppositions:
Gemini-Sagittarius:

Wisdom versus knowledge, wickedness versus goodness, reason versus instinct, college versus University, short distance journeys versus, long-distance journeys. With this pair, people are concerned with education, sharing information and travel. This combination in people's chart shows that they are very much interested in everything that is talkative, and they want to accomplish as much as they can in their lives. Gemini represents the exemplary student, because he or she wants to know everything; while Sagittarius loves to teach, and therefore, processes the knowledge. And, of course, Gemini represents a young child who will constantly ask "why?", apart from Sagittarius who is more concerned with morals, wisdom and judgment; and both will stay youthful in this spirit.

Virgo-Pisces:

Blame versus sympathy, order versus disorder, flawlessness versus completeness, judgment versus state of being. Individuals with this polarity are flexible and they are concerned with service. With this combination, the individual is a genuinely a kind person. Virgo is interested in providing hands on service to others, while Pisces are rather selfless and will sacrificed much, due to their devotion to others. But, as a pair: they would remain humble and show great kindness towards others. People with this pair often can be victimized or they may take on the role of being the savior. They love to rescue or they want to be rescued. Virgo has the belief that every situation and issue should be examined clearly and thoroughly, until the right answer is found. But, on the other hand, this is not the concern of Pisces: but is only interested in comparative values. Pisces will go with the flow, but Virgo concerns itself with others and improving the self.

Mutable-squares:
Gemini-Virgo:

These signs are naturally squared of each other, and they have a great deal in common. Virgo is an airy earth sign, and in this pair; it is confronting an air sign. Most importantly, both signs are ruled by Mercury. It is pointing to the fact that individuals who have this pair dominated in their charts may have difficulty in keeping focus. People with tight squares between Gemini and Virgo are critical, irritable and quick to find fault. With Mercury ruling, there can be talents in language, and they are well learned. They may also, come across as though they know it all. When they are stirred with a sense of direction, this pair will put them in all forms of study. This can work best in anything that has to do with sorting detailed information and gathering and categorizing them.

Gemini-Pisces:

This combination is mild, and it is restless. Gemini is a lucid sign, and it is concerned with ideas, learning new knowledge, and facts. However, Pisces is more concerned with morals than ideas and is not concerned with the facts. People who have this square stressed in their chart may experience a struggle between what is real and what is not. And, they want to bring the reality of the outer world and inner world into proper alignment. Also, with Mercury being well placed in your chart, you will be able do creative imaginative writing, especially poetry. Gemini and Pisces people feel inundated with a number of images and ideas that floats through their minds. The things that they cannot understand, ultimately, are what they try to over rationalize to gain a better understanding. They love to talk things through.

Virgo-Sagittarius:

This pair normally have all the talkativeness and can be restless, which is more than can be expected from a mutable combination. Virgo is much concerned with the details of everyday life, while Sagittarius is never bothered with the niceties. If the squares are accentuated in an individual's chart, he or she can make mountains out of molehills. They tend to be overly critical about other people's imperfections, also their own. Most of the criticism is directed towards other people's belief, and on some occasions their own. On the other hand, this can be used for analyzing different beliefs and thoughts, and for working in this field of philosophy. They will be able to work as counselors, psychologists, social workers, and legal counselors. Your philosophy about life is more to serve than be served, and you will work well in an organization.

Sagittarius-Pisces:

People with this combination are mostly yearning for their idealism. They are great travelers in the imagination, if they don't do it in reality. They also fantasize a lot, if Uranus has a strong influence in the chart. Neither of the signs likes to be confined in any way. Sagittarius-Pisces can be optimism and would always keep the door open, because they tend to believe that something magical can happened. You can become quite restless, and will experience a great deal of dissatisfaction. Because of this, you can become a drifter. Sagittarius usually gives spirit to Pisces, and in turn: Pisces will refine Sagittarius enthusiasm. People with this combination can have an innocent and dubious feeling, but they are easy-going. When these signs are squared, there may be internal conflicts with your political and religious views: and may find that they are at odds with the environment and will make the adjustments.

The Bible and Astrology:

The Bible is full of astrology, but the secrets components of the Bible have been demonized by many. It represents the passage of man through Christ, and how the secrets can be unfolded. However, the Bible is purposely and tactically intertwined with astrological roots. From time to time, the facts present itself through someone who is radical enough to share it with the world, so that you can understand the mysteries of God. The typical theologian (preacher), fundamentalist Christian, and the traditional believers, will find this to be offensive.

But, when you look at the Bible in its purest form, you will find that it has far more value than one would ever imagine. Unfortunately, what most people hold as truth turns out to be false evidence. Consequently, the Bible turns out to be the very first book of freedom and liberation. When you know how to understand the Bible, you would know how to understand yourself. But, you must break free from mental slavery, before you can embrace the truths: because they were purposely hidden from you to keep you uninformed and powerless. Remember, when you apply knowledge: you have the power.

In fact, there is a limited amount of people who have any concept or understands how the Bible was put together. There were approximately 47 scholars who were commissioned by his Majesty King James I to translate the Bible. Who wrote the rules and principles and what they should follow, so one can infer that the Bible was really translated by him. He wanted the new version to be conformed to ecclesiology and reflect the Episcopal of the Church of England. All of the scholars were members of the church. Consequently, the truths that were hidden in the Bible: so it can lead people to oppression and bondage, if they do not unlock them and try to understand them.

To understand how the Bible is full of astrological signs: one must understand the birth of Christ. It represents light (knowledge) to overcome the darkness (ignorance). Before there was a Bible, a Koran, a Torah: God was, and still is. Man received messages of accuracy from God through the heavens. *The heavens declare the glory of God; and the firmament sheweth his handiwork." Psalm 19:1.* When Christ was found, he was found through the system and the stars, which was astrology. *"Now when Jesus was born in Bethlehem of Judea in the days of Herod the King, behold there, came wise men from the east to Jerusalem. Saying, where is He that is born King of the Jews? For we have seen His star in the east, and are come to worship Him." Matthew 2:1-2 (KJV)*

There are many scriptures in the Bible that deals with astrology, because everything in the Bible is there for a reason. Isaiah the prophet: give reference to astrologers as counselors. In Isaiah 47:13,: *Thou wearied in the multitude of thy counsels. Let now the astrologers, the stargazers, the monthly prognosticators, and stand up, and save these things that shall came upon thee".* However, God does not condemn astrologers for practicing astrology, but would condemn others for coming up against his people. In the Scripture above, Isaiah senses that the astrologers would be able to save the things (knowledge) of God.

However, when God declared that there should be lights, He was referring to the stars which have to do with astrology. In Genesis 1:14, *"and God said, let there be lights in the firmament of the heaven to divide the day from the night; and let them be for signs, and for seasons, and for days, and years."* Astrology is the study of the stars and how they communicate with us. When you look at the word light, for example, it is

132

referring to the planets, which are considered to be constellations. These stars make up the zodiac.

The stars are there to be signs, so that we can understand the mysteries of God. *"And there shall be signs in the sun, and in the moon, and in the stars; and upon the earth distress of nations, with perplexity: the sea and the waves roaring. Men's hearts failing them for fear, and for looking after those things which are coming on the earth: for the powers of heaven shall be shaken. And then shall they see the Son of man coming in a cloud with power and great glory. And when these things begin to come to pass, then look up, and lift up your heads; for your redemption draweth nigh. And he spake to them a parable: Behold the fig tree, and all the trees; when they now shoot forth, ye see and know of your own selves that summer is now nigh at hand. So likewise ye, when ye see these things come to pass, know ye that the kingdom of God is nigh at hand. Verily I say unto you, This generation shall not pass away, till all be fulfilled."* Luke 21: 25-32

The stars are there for a specific purpose, and not just to decorate the sky, and they are there for astrologers to study and interpret them. They give deeper meaning to events of the past and will in turn give information about things to come. But, God is the one who is controlling the heavenly bodies, and not man. The stars are being used as His instrument to give us clear and precise directions. Furthermore, in Genesis 49, the twelve sons of Jacob are a relevant sign to that of the zodiac. Jacob was preparing to die, so he gathered his sons, so that he can give unto them the prophetic word, concerning their lives. And, of course, he used symbolic language to compare each of his sons to that of the zodiac.

The 12 Tribes of Israel	Astrological Symbolism
Judah	Leo ♌
Zebulun	Pisces ♓
Issachar	Taurus

	♉
Dan	Scorpio ♏
Rueben	Aquarius ♒
Simeon	Capricorn ♑
Gad	Aries ♈
Benjamin	Sagittarius ♐
Asher	Libra ♎
Naphtali	Virgo ♍
Levi	Gemini ♊
Joseph	Cancer

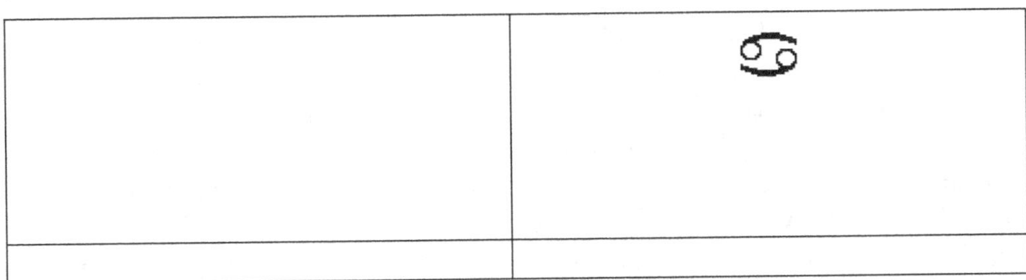

As an illustration, Jesus is considered to be known as the bright and Morning Star. He is referred to in songs that we sing in church, which is directly connected to astrology. Revelation 22:16 says *"I Jesus have sent mine angel to testify unto you these things in the churches. I am the root and offspring of David, and the bright and morning star."* And in 2 Peter 1:19, *"We have also a more sure word of prophecy; whereunto ye do well that ye take heed, as unto a light shineth in a dark place, until the dawn, and the day star arise in your hearts."* The interesting things is: astrology is being sung in the churches daily, so in a sense: the traditional Christians are helping to share astrology with their congregations, on a weekly basis.

The purpose of astrology and how it is used in the Bible is to help to guide you, and give you insights into things that may not be visible to you. There really isn't anything wrong in trying to find out the hidden things about yourself, because you will be able to know where you are going in life. Astrologers were assigned to Kings and Queens, so that they can better understand how to rule their kingdom. They understood the necessity and need for an astrologer. Joseph interpreted a dream for Pharaoh, which can be inferred that he used astrology to interpret it, to give him directions. (Genesis 41)

Daniel was considered to be a master magician, because he was the only one who could have interpreted the dream for King Nebuchadnezzar. *"O Belteshazzar, master of the magicians, because I know that the spirit of the holy gods is in thee, and no secret troubleth thee, tell me the visions of my dream that I have seen, and the interpretation thereof. Then Daniel, whose name was Belteshazzar, was astonied for one hour."* Daniel 4:9, 19.

Phases of the Moon:

135

The Moon has different phases because it orbits the Earth and its appearance changes over time. The portion that we see is illuminated. It takes 27.3 day to orbit, but the lunar phase cycle, which is new Moon to new Moon, takes 29.5 days to orbit. It is easiest to understand the moon cycle in this manner: new moon, full moon, first quarter, third quarter, and the phases in between. However, the Moon spends an extra 2.2 days to catch up. If two full Moons occur in one month, it is considered to be a blue moon, which normally happens every three years. Because Earth's gravity has slowed down the rational speed of the Moon, we can only see a specific side of it.

The effects of the Moon are shown in the ocean tides. The angle of the ecliptic, which is the Moon's path across the sky, gives the visibility of the Moon. The Moon moves almost parallel to the horizon as it rises, when the ecliptic is at low angle to the horizon. However, the position of the Sun and the Earth normally gives the Moon the different phases. The cycle is a continuous process, which are: New Moon, Waxing Crescent Moon, Quarter Moon (first quarter), Waxing Gibbous Moon, Full Moon, Waning Gibbous Moon, Last or Third Quarter Moon, and Waning crescent Moon.

The new Moon was represented by Diana, in Roman mythology, the hunter goddess. It also represents the feeling nature of the individual, because it is connected to the emotional make-up of the unconscious habits, memories, moods, and rhythms. Also, there is an association with the mother (the maternal instincts) and the need to nurture, the home and the past. It is also use to illustrate the inner child in each of us, as well as the past and how we were as individuals, then and now. The way in, which one perceives his or her mother, can also be connected to the Moon. It also represents the directness and susceptibility of the individual. For arguments sake, the Moon has power, because it can be considered be equals with the Sun, and there is a hidden mysterious and influential power that lies within the Moon.

"Mythologically, the Moon was personified as the Goddess, and in her triple form she displayed herself at Artemis the new moon, Selene the full moon, and Hecate the dark moon. These symbolized the maiden, mother, and crone phases of a woman's life span." (Bloch, & George, 2006 p. 56) Since the Moon is tied to emotions, it is believed that it represents the woman. The woman is more the nurturer of the family and

136

she goes through different cycles and phases, as well. It is also considered to be the foundation for other planets, and represents the fullness of time. Our emotional needs are tied within the Moons, and the things that we cannot do without.

Also, it is a exemplification of the Yin and offers itself as the receptive one that gives usage of the Sun's energy, and helps to bring things into manifestation. Everyone will be able to actualize the potential of the Sun, by utilizing the personality of the Moon; this must be done from within our being. Our patterns and daily habits along with our concepts are all associated with the Moon's energy. This will help us to be nurturing and receptive to others. The Moon is also responsible for the changing conditions of the environment, so that man can adjust how he relates to the world.

The Moon has the ability to be flexible, and it can provoke this within us, so that we would learn how to unfold the Sun's purpose; making our responses instinctive because it is a part of our emotional reactions. This is the experiences from our childhood, and the relationships with family members. It has an influence on us, during the earliest part of our life, because our minds are emotional devices and they are being developed. This is how we absorb our parents' attitudes. This gives growth to our psychological patterns which helps to form our personality.

Because the Moon is the ruler of a water sign, it rules our emotional life through our feelings. It does not recognize when something is separated from us. On the other hand, when our world is combined with feeling, we become intuitive and can perceive things beyond cogent knowing. But, we cannot allow our unstable emotions to become too excessive, because we will only ride on an emotional roller coaster; which will be at the mercy of our ever altering moods. The Moon also oversees the past. However, we can have access to our personal subconscious, cultural memory and our familial heritage, through the Moon. The Moon rules the menstrual cycle, the mother's milk, and the body fluids, among other things. It ushers the woman into her womanhood.

New Moon:

This Moon is the lunar phase, in astronomical terms, which occurs when it is in its monthly orbital motion around the Earth, and it takes place over the western horizon between sunset and moonset. This can be termed as a conjunction with the Sun. During this time, the dark (unilluminated) portion of the Moon is, almost directly, facing the Earth, and therefore, the Moon would not be visible to the naked eye. However, this Moon can also be known as the astronomically dark Moon, and it transpires at the moment of conjunction of the ecliptic longitude with the Sun, when the Moon is invisible from the Earth. This is, actually, a very unique moment, and location has nothing to do with it. The New Moon is the beginning of the month in lunar calendars, but in the Chinese calendars: it is termed as the dark Moon.

It is also considered that people that are born in this first quarter (new Moon) can have an essential sense of youthful enthusiasm and optimism. These people normally take the initiative, especially when it comes to romance, which of course, make them ready for new interests in life. It is easy for them to view things in a productive manner, and what needs to be improved, so that they can shoot others into taking action. They tend to get off to an early start in life with much success. Furthermore, the date and time of the new Moon solely depends on the geographical location of the observer. The new Moon plays a great role in the Hindu calendar.

New Moon in the Hindu culture:

In Indian (Jyotisa or Vedic) astrology, the new Moon is called Chandra, and can be identified with the deity Soma. He is said to be the god of the Moon, and is believed that when the Moon is waned, the gods have drank all of the Soma, and when it is waxed, the gods are recreating themselves. The Hindu has a myth about the new Moon, which one of it is: they start new work after the new Moon day. There is also a rotation of the calendar (panchang or panchanga), which starts from the first day date and ends on the sixth day date. Furthermore, the new Moon can be quite significant in the Hindu calendar, and the people tend to wait for it, before starting any networks.

New Moon in the Chinese culture:

In many different religious bodies, the use of the New Moon can have different meaning and use, especially in the Chinese culture. Some of the Chinese (Buddhist) people maintain a vegetarian diet on the day of the new Moon. The Moon is associated with the Yin (mother) side, and the Chinese god of the Earth. It is considered that the new Moon is the awakening, the renewal, sowing, and the birth of an individual. They examine everything that was started, during the new Moon to make sure that they are on the right path. The new Moon falls between the beginning of January and February, which is when the Chinese year falls.

In the Chinese calendar (lunisolar), there are 12 lunar months, except for the leap year, which has 13 months: and the first day of the month is considered to be the new Moon. The months that the new Moon falls in have names of animals. The Moon houses have 28 mansions, which are divided into four segments. The Chinese New Year: which is celebrated on new Moon of the first month is a time for reunions, feasts, and family. This is the most important celebration in the Chinese culture. At this time, they leave all their problems from the previous year behind, so that they can embrace the new things. They clean their house, and buy new clothes in order for everything to be fresh and new around them.

New Moon in the Jewish culture:

In the Jewish culture, the people also have faith in the new Moon, as well. Their calendar is similar to that of the Chinese calendar. The Jewish community has placed a deep concern for this day, and they have a holiday on the Hebrew calendar for it. It also starts the Jewish month, which is the most essential date in the Jewish calendar. The new Moon is very important, because it is needed for the Jewish holidays: they revolve around the date of the new Moon. It helps to reveal the Midrash, which is seen as a great spiritual power that is granted to the children of Israel. They have a belief that they are the only ones who can make the Moon holy, and the holidays holy.

Additionally, some of the Rabbis believed that the blessings for consecrating the new Moon are: "Blessed are You Hashem, Who makes the Children of Israel holy." To keep the universe in existence, they believe that the effect of bringing the holiness into the world is the gateway for this, and by continuously renewing it. In the Jewish culture, it is also believed that the new Moon is what keeps the month holy. Another interested thing is: that they believe that when they sanctify the Moon, they will know when the holiday will be. The phases of the Moon teach them a valuable lesson, which is no one is perfect, and that it does not gives us: because it comes back every month.

139

The waxing crescent Moon:

The waxing crescent Moon, also known as the young Moon is usually seen in the west after sunset. It is far away from Earth and the Sun, and it will be seen after sunset. This Moon can be seen anywhere from one day to a few days, after the new Moon. During these days, the Moon rises approximately one hour to several hours behind the sun, and it follows the sun across the sky, during the course of the day. After the sun sets and the sky darkens, the Moon pops into the sky into view in the western sky. Depending on one's geographical location, it will be able to be seen. The crescent Moon; however, has nothing to do with the Earth's shadow on the Moon. The shadow that is on this Moon is the Moon's shadow. There is a pale glow on the night side of the crescent Moon, which is the glow that is reflected from the Earth's day side, which is called the earthshine.

The waxing crescent in the Hindu culture:

In the Hindu culture, their belief is that every living being has a soul, and that every soul is divine, because it has inborn qualities of infinite knowledge. They are born with power and know how to utilize their perception with bliss. One of their essential beliefs is that every soul is born to a heavenly being and would express itself through the karma. There are principles that are attached to their beliefs and they savor the Moon for the wisdom that they believe comes from it. The Waxing Crescent is a symbol that is used by Hindus and is considered a lamp of heaven. This symbol of the Waxing Crescent Moon is on the forehead of Bhairava and Mahakala, two of their gods. This symbolizes the rebirth aspect of the Moon and feminine power and their womanhood.

The waxing crescent in the Jewish culture:

In the Jewish culture, the Waxing Crescent symbolizes the beginning of a new cycle of creation. Their celebration begins when the Moon is far away from the Sun so that it appears as a crescent in the western sky. One of their beliefs during this Moon phase is to cast bread crumbs into the sea and moving water will release the sins of the past year. The crescent Moon is called the "Rosh Hodesh" .

The first quarter Moon:

The quarter moon only shows half of the lighted hemisphere, the day side, to Earth. It is called the quarter moon, because it is a quarter way around the orbit of the Earth. However, on the night of the Moon, half of the Moon's day side is seen: thus making another lighted quarter of the Moon shine brightly in the direction of the Earth. It rises at noon, and is at the highest point at sunset: and it sets at midnight. This quarter Moon comes a week after the new Moon. At the right angles to a line between the Earth and sun the Moon is in its orbit.

The waxing gibbous Moon:

The waxing Gibbous Moon normally appears high in the east, at sunset, and it is more half-lighted, and it is less full. It has moved in its orbit, and it is now far from the sun. This Moon rises during noon and sunset, and it sets in the early hours after midnight. It can also be seen in the afternoon, depending on your geographical location. This happens when the sun is descending in the west, while the waxing Gibbous is ascending in the east. During this time, a large fraction of the Moon day side is facing our way; and it is more noticeable in the sky, rather than a crescent Moon. Furthermore, it is further from the sun on the sky's dome, and the sun's glare is not hiding its view.

The full Moon:

The full Moon is a lunar phase that occurs when the Moon is on the opposite side of the Earth. This actually takes place when the ecliptic longitude of the sun and the Moon differs by 180 degrees. This is when the Moon and the Sun is in opposition of each other, and the Earth is in between. It is fully illuminated by the sun and it is reflecting the light of the sun, which appears round. The opposite side of the Moon (the far side) is only completely illuminated during a full Moon. The full Moon falls approximately on the 14th or15th of each month. The full Moon rises when the sun set and is most visible, and sets when the sun rises.

The full Moon is considered to be opposite of the new Moon. It is in line with the Earth and sun, and it comes approximately two weeks after the new Moon. A lunar eclipse only takes place, during the phase of the full Moon. Consequently, there is a misleading mindset that the full Moon has a duration of a full night, because the Moon, when seen from on Earth is becoming larger or smaller. But, this cannot be seen with the naked eyes. At the moment when expansion stops, and the tangent slope is zero: it reaches its maximum size. The full Moon can mostly be seen from any given location. The full Moon can also be known for the blue Moon, and

141

they are considered to be sacred to Buddhist tradition. If a season has four full Moons, this is considered to be a blue Moon.

Full Moon in the Hindu culture:

Purnima or Poornima is how full Moon is called in the Hindu culture. This is a highly auspicious day and there is a fast during this time, which is from sunset to sunset. The Moon is considered to be a god and bears its significance, which of course; there are rituals that are done on this day. Some people only have food after they see the Moon or after their evening prayers. This celebration welcomes in joy and happiness to those who follow the tradition. Just before the full Moon (the Chhoti) people gather at major cross roads on the streets and start a bonfire, which is called Holika Dahan.

They give thanks to the god of fire (Agni) for all the blessings that they have received, during the year. They believe that the bon fire's ashes that are collected during the full Moon can protect them from evil forces, because they see the full Moon as a period of endings of one phase, and the beginning of a new phase. According to their Vedic philosophies: when the Moon is in Virgo: there is a tendency to be indecisive or have confusion, while one is trying to be logical. Within the Hindu culture, there is a mantra that is recited during this time (Om Eim Saraswatiyei Swaha). The common belief is that it invokes new energies for making any projects fruitful and successful; and when Mercury in in retrograde, this should be recited until the next full Moon.

Full Moon in the Chinese culture:

The Chinese culture is deeply imbedded in traditional festivals. The Moon event is one of the most important one for Chinese. It is full of legendary stories, and one of them is: Chang Er flew to the Moon and was saved and is now living there. During their Moon festival, they believe that she dances on the Moon. This is also an occasion for family reunions, because when the full Moon rises, families get together to watch the Moon. They eat moon cakes and sing moon poems. The Moon festival is also a romantic time for lovers, and for couples who cannot be together: each person watches the Moon at the same time, so that they can be brought together at least for an hour.

At this time, romantic partners write poems to each other, and hope that the Moon festival will being them happiness. They also do a Lion dance to celebrate the full Moon. This festival came from the Tang Dynasty, when the Moon is at its fullest. This festival is similar to the American Thanksgiving holiday, because they celebrate a bountiful harvest, and they use a lot of vibrant colors to display their excitement. To make the festival more personal and special, Chinese people celebrate it outside under the moonlight, while eating the traditional delicacies. This celebration takes place on the 15th of August, yearly.

Full Moon in the Jewish culture:

The Jewish calendar is not the same length as the western world calendar. It is based on three astronomical phenomena, which is how the Earth rotates on its axis (day), the revolution of the Moon and the Earth (a month), and the revolution of the Earth about the sun (a year). And, all three are totally dependent on each other. Their month begins with a silver moon, which become visible after the dark moon.

The Jewish calendar has the following months:

Hebrew	English	Number	Length	Civil Equivalent
נִיסָן	Nissan	1	30 days	March-April
אַיָּיר	Iyar	2	29 days	April-May
סִיוָן	Sivan	3	30 days	May-June
תַּמּוּז	Tammuz	4	29 days	June-July
אָב	Av	5	30 days	July-August
אֱלוּל	Elul	6	29 days	August-September
תִּשְׁרִי	Tishri	7	30 days	September-October
חֶשְׁוָן	Cheshvan	8	29 or 30 days	October-November
כִּסְלֵו	Kislev	9	30 or 29 days	November-December

143

טֵבֵת	Tevet	10	29 days	December-January
שְׁבָט	Shevat	11	30 days	January-February
אֲדָר א	Adar I (leap years only)	12	30 days	February-March
אֲדָר / אֲדָר ב	Adar (called Adar Beit in leap years)	12 (13 in leap years)	29 days	February-March

Furthermore, the length of Cheshvan and Kislev are determined by the calculations which involves the day of the full Moon. The calendar is rooted in cycles of the moon. Also, they recite a blessing over the moon in gratitude for having been given the cycles of life. Their days are named differently to that of the western calendar, as well.

Hebrew	Transliteration	English
יוֹם רִשׁוֹן	Yom Rishon	First Day (Sunday)
יוֹם שֵׁינִי	Yom Sheini	Second Day (Monday)
יוֹם שְׁלִישִׁי	Yom Shlishi	Third Day (Tuesday)
יוֹם רְבִיעִי	Yom R'vi'i	Fourth Day (Wednesday)
יוֹם חֲמִישִׁי	Yom Chamishi	Fifth Day (Thursday)
יוֹם שִׁשִׁי	Yom Shishi	Sixth Day (Friday)
יוֹם שַׁבָּת	Yom Shabbat	Sabbath Day (Saturday)

The full Moon is known as Keseh, which is the 15th of the Hebrew month. They believe that the full Moon is like a brimming cup of abundance. The full Moon also signals a time when the divine womb creates pure and blessed souls. At this time, the Sun and the Moon represents the masculine and feminine aspect of God.

The waning gibbous Moon:

A few days after the full Moon, the waning Gibbous can be seen in the west, early in the morning floating against the soft blue sky over the

144

eastern horizon between sunset and midnight. It is past full in this state, and it will appear less than full, and more than half lighted. It rises after sunset, and it glows red like a full Moon, when it is near the horizon. It comes up late at night, and people may look for it, because they may be able to see it, it can also been seen during the day.

Third or last quarter Moon:

The last quarter Moon looks half illuminated, and it rises around midnight, and at dawn: it appears to be highest in the sky, and it sets at noon. It normally occurs three weeks after new Moon in its orbit around the Earth. The last quarter Moon is at the right angle to a line between the Earth and the sun. In this position, it is three quarters of the way around in the orbit of the Earth. On the sky's dome, the Moon will be noticeably closer to the sun. The sun's glare dominates the Moon, during last quarter: so fewer people will notice it during the day. It can also be used as a guidepost to the Earth, while it is orbiting the sun.

The waning crescent Moon:

The waning crescent is also called an old Moon, which is seen before dawn, in the east. The day hemisphere is away from us, because the Moon is nearly on a line with the Earth and the Sun. There is only a fraction of it that can be seen. The Moon appears closer to the sunrise each morning, while moving eastward in the orbit around the Earth, which gives the crescent in the east before dawn appears. This can only be seen early in the morning: because the sun makes the sky too clear to see the waning crescent. And, it will set in the west hours before the sunset. This Moon represents the removal of troubles, expelling of old habits, and casting out of old ways. However, the word waning means decreasing in size, and Gibbous means that more than one half of the surface is illuminated.

Interpretation of my chart:

The natal chart (astrological chart) is a symbolic representation of the position of the planets in a person's chart. "A birth chart is the individual symbolical macrocosmic representation of the potential fullness of the perfected microcosm. It is the blue-print of the complete man." (Rudhyar, 1970 p.391). It helps to provide insights into a person's personality and behavior. They are based on facts that are more of an astronomical endeavor to gain more information about the individual.

145

Because astrology is a study of the celestial bodies, the positions of the planets would be analyzed based on their positions in the individual's natal chart.
Elements:
Antoinette John. Monday May 25th, 1964
Fire: 2
Earth: 6
Water: 3
Modes: Cardinal: 1
Fixed: 4
Mutable: 7

Planet and houses:

It is important to know how the chart is created, so that it can give a deeper meaning to the individual. "Truly, a chart erected for a particular time and location on the Earth's surface pictures for us *the archetypal character of whatever is born then and there.* But in natal astrology, at least from a humanistic point of view, we are dealing with abstract forms." (Rudhyar, 1980 p.304) Ascendant, is at 01 degrees, is in Sagittarius (Mutable Fire, Ruler Planet: Jupiter), and the Moon, 00 degrees, is also in Sagittarius. The South Node (03 degrees) is in the second house which is in Capricorn, while Saturn is (04 degrees) in the fourth house (Pisces, Mutable water). Taurus has three planets (Mercury 09 degrees, Jupiter 10 degrees, and Mars 13 degrees, along with the path of fortune 26 degrees (6th house). Gemini (Mutable air) has the Sun (04 degrees, and is the 7th house), and Cancer has the North Node (03 degrees, and Venus 06 degrees (8th house). Virgo has The Midheaven (02 degrees, Uranus 05 degree, and Pluto 11 degrees) which is the 10th house. In the 12th house (Scorpio), Neptune is at 15 degrees.

Moon and ascendant in Sagittarius:

The Moon ties in with emotions, feelings and the daily routine. It also defines the female aspect, which is tied in with the Yin. The Moon also helps the individual to be at home with oneself. "Mythologically, the Moon was personified as the Goddess, and in her triple form she displayed herself as Artemis the new moon." (Blooch, & George, 2006 p. 56) Giving is not a problem, but it is important that people are thankful when things are given to them. Sagittarius is a mutable fire sign and I normally react enthusiastically based on the things that I do believe in. It is easy to be

146

contended when she is promoting my beliefs and principles. Once I believe in something, it is hard to persuade me, otherwise.

Nothing or no one will detour her when I am moving towards my goals. Loves to question things, so that a meaning can be reached; this is important; because this way knowledge can become available. There is a comfortable feeling when traveling and exploring; loves outdoor activities. With the Moon ruling a water sign, there is a deep sense of feeling, and emotions run deep. Loves to socialize and be the life of the party; and expressing the self is not taken for granted, since this is something that brings liberation to the mind. Being free is very important to this individual, because she does not like to feel cooped up. With the Moon and the Ascendant in Sagittarius, this individual will have close relationships with women, and maintain close emotional relationships with people who he or she has known for a long time.

The Sun:

The sun is in the sign of Gemini, which is mutable air, and it shows creative energy; because they are thinkers and love creative expression. Loves to acquire facts and ask questions, so that the idea and make connections with it. Loves to express the self verbally and the individual can be motivated by intellectual concepts. Knows how to recharge energy through social interactions and involvement, which will help to stimulate intellectual ideas. Need to receive recognition for intellectual abilities. Have a wide variety of interests, and love to share ideas with others.

Planets in the signs:

There are three planets in Taurus, which is fixed earth sign, and if you pay attention to the degrees of the planets, you will notice that they are all in conjunct with each other. When planets are conjunct with each other, they share their energies and they will have a mutual change of energy and how they affect the individual. "In most charts, one or more planets are so heavily emphasized that they become keynotes in the individual's life." (Cunningham, 1999 p. 65) With Mercury in Taurus, the individual will communicate ideas, and thoughts very carefully, and giving much thought before actually speaking. The mind is usually steady, and based on a merging of ideas. Mercury deals with how the individual thinks and communicates.

147

Jupiter is the planet that attributes to how an individual grows, and seeks to improve the self, so this individual will strive to grow and expand in everything, but will need to feel secure and grounded about the decisions to grow. It is important to make connections with a larger order and an appreciation of the physical world. One of the ways to improve the self is through making the amount of money that she feels is desirable. This individual has a broad understanding of human nature and the needs of others. The relationship between Mercury and Mars depicts a unique way of expression anger or conflict. Loves to debate or argue a point, especially when the individual is right.

This individual is very energetic and dynamic in the thinking abilities. Also, there is a determination to act upon her ideas. There is a forceful way of using intellectual abilities. However, with Mercury and Jupiter: there is a strong sense of ability to make judgments with maximum understanding. This individual will love to negotiate and do business; expansion is very important to this individual. This individual will make a very good mediator, because fairness is important; and would look at the situation on both sides. Furthermore, the relationship between Mars and Jupiter is a bit rambunctious, and the individual will take action that will lead to growth.

Mars, Jupiter, and Mercury all have something in common. Mars has the drive, but the person can be stubborn, but the individual loves simple pleasures. It is important to the individual that he or she seeks to grow and improve through change through change and desire of compulsion, which complemented through life's changes.

Timing will bring luck to this individual, which will help to bring expansion. One of the ways that this individual will be able to have expansion will be through doing creative things, which will bring opportunities, especially in business. Venus is in Cancer, which is a water sign, and is ruled by the Moon. This individual can be very emotional, especially for others. Furthermore, this individual will be able to express the self in a sensitive and comforting manner. There is a strong need to nurture or be nurtured, and to be a part of a family. Yearns to share energy with people in an enclosed environment, but, the need for pleasure and closeness can be hampered by moodiness. The relationship with Venus and the North Node there is a love connection with others.

148

Love to meet with friends and people that are considered to be beautiful in spirit. This individual will love to work with artistic and creative people to achieve a creative objective. Virgo is an Earth sign and it is ruled by Mercury, and Pluto in this sign represents the need to have power, transformation, and death and rebirth of things that need to be buried or give birth to. On the other hand, Virgo is very analytical and grounded; very detailed oriented, intelligent, fussy, and bright. The individual can be very transparent (see me for who I am), and together with Uranus it gives the individual the opportunity to make great changes, by changing the methods of operation.

How the daily routine is dealt with a very important, but anything that is outdated will be taken out of the plan. Neptune is in fixed water (Scorpio), and this individual will have dreamy like qualities, because Neptune tends to be fixated on their dreams. The individual dreams about goals and achieving them, and how they would be achieved, but the goals can be dreamt about from the end, and how it will impact, so that it can either be aborted or fulfilled. Can be very secretive and understands the self. Love and romance is very important to this individual

Neptune is in opposition at 15 degrees, and when planets are in opposition: they know how to interact with each other, and they know how to move obstacles out of the way. It is easy to bring balance and confrontation, because they are directly in opposition. They will know how to oppose each other, because they know how to support each other, and how to deal with partnerships. This individual can be misunderstood, because she yearns for the mystical things of life. There is little tolerance for drama, and love to feel emotionally secure.

The Rising Sun (Ascendant) symbolizes how one reacts in the world and the image and personality of the individual. There is a spontaneous energy towards life that permeates the entire being. Furthermore, the image that others see may not be intended, but it is projected anyway: because it is automatic. It shows something essential about the individual. Because it is in the first house, it deals with the way in, which the individual views the self and deal with the personality. Physical appearance is of importance to the person, and how other perceive her will give a clear indication how the self is projected.

With the Ascendant in a fire sign, this individual will have a vast amount of energy, and have an optimistic outlook on life. Honesty is one of the traits of this individual and people may find that the individual is bluntly honest, which some may not appreciate. Very action oriented, and has a positive outlook on life. Very optimistic and enthusiastic individual, and possess a broad mind and can be inspiring and will take definite action with an epitome.

Planets in the houses:

Saturn is in the fourth house, which deals with the intimate life of the individual, and how the childhood and adulthood may have an impact on the individual. It also deals with the relationship that one has with the parents and native land. Everything that is kept inward; the things that are not shared with anyone are kept secret to the individual. With Saturn in the fourth house, it reveals how the individual understands the self and how aware the individual is of the self or others are. It is important to deal with matters immediately. There is a need to belong to something or someone, so that a support system can be formed.

With Saturn in Pisces, which is a mutable water sign, it makes it easy to adapt and organize things; there may be some restrictions; however, but this would not detour this individual, in any way. Loves rich things and how they tend to beautify the home and the self.

Mercury, Mars, and Jupiter are all in the sixth house and this deals with service, employees, nutrition and hygiene. Serving gives an instant

gratification. There can also be "Deception by women ☿ in 6th House GA053" (Lehman, 1992 p. 73) There are activities that are pursued, but not for the self, but for the sake of something else. Saturn energy will be responsible for human happiness, which is something that the individual is seeking. Jupiter's energy for expansion, success and achievement is shown in the individual's desire for success, and in the things that are achieved. The thing that moves the individual, especially in the psyche is attached to the energies of Jupiter. It also represents how one reaches out to others.

Mars displays a very energetic individual, and how one exists in something that is bigger than the self. The energy is very individualistic, and it is important how differences are emphasized with similarities. There is a survival energy that helps to embody the self-centeredness in the individual which will help to highlight the differences in the individual. If there is any aggression, there may be the reason for "fight or flight" reaction, since the individual will do what is best for her and others who are connected to her.

The seventh house deals with relations, marriage, and partnerships. How one acts and feels in a relationship and how the other person who is in the relationship feels. "So the seventh house planets show you what you're looking for in a relationship and, most importantly, they show what parts of yourself you will get in touch with through close relationships." (1993 p. 29) This chart is depicting that the other half in the relationship would be seen, someone in the public eyes. How the two can become one is very important to the individual. Very romantic, yet seeks intimacy, which is something that is unique in a marriage. Also, the chart is describing my partner, lover, helpmate, and friend. He is someone who loves to be seen and since it is conjunct with Venus, Midheaven, Uranus, Ascendant, Saturn, and the North and South Nodes.

He loves expansion, and to achieve his goals. His self-image is very important, and he would go to great lengths to maintain it. He is a very loving individual, and will take charge in life to take care of his family. Doing internal cleansing through meditating will help him to overcome challenges. It's in the tenth house, so his career would be one that brings honor to him. For the chart as to how it deals with the individual, the tenth house shows that the individual will be pushed into the spotlight suddenly, and how the mind deals with this sudden move. The role that is being played in society is very important, and how the energies are projected.

The North Nodes is in Cancer, which makes the individual more nurturing, but with Venus, it accentuates the social aspects and how the individual relates to the people in her life. Also, it emphasizes how she learns things and how others learn in their own time. Meaning: she does not expect a kindergartener to know calculus, but she knows what is taught to her. Have a love for knowledge and loves to share it with those who welcome it. Rather than nurturing directly, it is more of being "free to be me" and accepting people for who they are.

Elements in the chart:

There are six earth elements (planets), which would make this individual very grounded. In Taurus, there are three planets (Mercury, Jupiter, and Mars); this individual would be very talkative, and will love to share ideas and information with others. Of course, this individual is very mindful of her thoughts, and loves to do in-depth thinking. However, with Jupiter in Taurus, it shows how the individual looks at things or value things in her life. Since it deals with faith, it is important that people are faithful to her; and likewise she is faithful to them, because it takes two to make things work. This individual is very fixed on her faith and beliefs, and since Jupiter is in an earth sign, it is impossible to shake her faith.

Also, Jupiter deals with expansion, it is important to know that there is room for growth, whether it is spiritual, emotional, or material, especially in finances. Everything that this individual does, she expects it to be great or to achieve success in doing such. She is very competitive, in the sense that there is an inner drive to win at whatever she does. Because Jupiter and Mercury is in the same sign, and they are one degree off of each other, neither of them is strengthen or weakened because they will share each other's energies. They will correlate with each other's aspects: giving room for expansive creative idea. They balance each other.

Furthermore, Jupiter is trapped between Mercury and Mars, and would be pushed in both directions. Mercury will make the individual very talkative, because it will accentuate the Sun quality. Mars will increase her willfulness in a certain way. That is where the confidence comes in from Jupiter, and will speak confidently about things and events. Mars adds force, which makes this individual someone who does not like injustice to anyone, and does not like to see advantage being taken on other people's kindness. People will know where they stand with this individual, but can be surprised of the way some people perceive her to be, especially those who she has a relationship with. The Mars-Jupiter also makes this individual very fearless.

Modes in the chart:

With the Cardinal modes, it shows that this person loves to take the lead, when doing this; she is an initiator. Venus is in Cancer, which is cardinal, makes it easy to have new and innovative ideas and concepts about new things. Also, this individual can be very mystical and spontaneous and somewhat impulsive, as well. However, the planets that are in fixed signs gives her the ability to follow through things to completion, and have the characteristics of a builder: very solid, stable,

152

loyal, consistent and can be stubborn, at times. The planets that are in the mutable signs make it easy to adapt and would know how to adjust to circumstances and things.

Also, it is easy to get around and knows how to utilize projects and bring them to completion. This individual can also start groups, by gathering members to implement change. There is also a burst of energy that is pertaining to this individual. A very highly mental individual; and once the mind grasp the need for change, it will be very easy to accommodate change and move with the flow. This person will seek to understand the environment, whether it is inner or outer. Will try to understand the inner being, so that what is on the outside can be a true demonstration on the inside, because whatever is around her will be comprehensive and would be able to adapt, having positive results.

However, the first elements show that this individual has a lot of energy, and if the individual is quiet, she can burst out in anger. With the energy of Mars and Jupiter, which is a natural ruler of a fire sign, this individual will have the characteristics of the fire signs. Mars energy can make this individual very argumentative, especially when she is right about things; loves to debate and win, of course. It is easy to let go of things, depending on the attachment and emotional ties; and knows how to ignore people. This individual loves to travel and explore things. This individual is very passionate about beautiful things in the home, artistic, and can be very nurturing to others, especially children.

Also, this individual is very friendly and warm to others, but if she feels betrayed or someone betrays her, she would walk away from that friendship, easily. Freedom is important to this individual, she loves to know that she can be free to express herself and go places. That is why she does not want a mate in the same sign, so that they can balance each other. Does not want to take advantage of the freedom, but loves to know that it is there.

Aspects in the chart:
Saturn squared in the Sun:

When Saturn is squared the Sun, the individual can be faced with a number of challenges in life, especially in the first half of it. There may be a feeling of persistency to get what the individual wants. There will be attempts made to control the environment, especially the inner environment; and does not like the feeling of inadequacy. Being accomplished and an important person are also important, and do not consider obstacles as an enemy; it only gives the opportunity to get past them. There is a longing for the world to consider this individual as important. Furthermore, there is a grave need of self-awareness to the point of real self-consciousness that it make the mystical things appear real.

Most importantly, this individual needs to stop worrying about always being right, and learn how to take the pressure off of the self, and ease the pressure that is placed on the self. It is all about what the individual feel is deserving, and if happiness and peace is some of the things that she feel that she deserve, then they would be a part of her experience. With the energy of the Sun, the parent within, which rules the conscious mind, it is important to gain an inner peace, so that things would be organized in a structured manner. With both Saturn and the Sun, there is much self-empowering that is going on, and the individual will analyze things carefully to make sure what should or shouldn't be done.

Saturn, like the parent within, will help to guide the thoughts to bring about a favorable outcome. It is like having the subconscious being censored. An important lesson that can be learned here is that the individual should not be too hard on the self, by setting standards that are too high. In order to avoid pitfalls in life, the paths that are too hard should not be chosen. There is a sense of humor, the ability to apply caution and strategy, and a keen intelligence. It is important for this individual to take care of teeth, bones, and the circulatory system, in order to maintain optimal health.

Saturn squared Uranus:

This individual loves security and inner peace. With Uranus, there is a sense of freedom that makes her feel safe, knowing that choices can be made. There is a strong sense of individuality and a feeling to be safe as an individual without having to compromise anything. It is not a good idea to be stuck in a job that the individual does not like, but to go after the desires of the heart. The things that are most believed in will be manifested, by this individual: and is creating it right now. Tension should not be created, and trust outer security, but what is within will help to bring about what is in the outer world. There is a strong need to be respected.

Saturn squared Pluto:

Pluto will unfold its wisdom to the individual, and things will come in a full circle. It is important not to resist its influences, but to work with it, because it is a planet of rebirth and destiny. When it touches different parts of the individual's life and psyche, it is easy for this individual to explore things deeply. With Pluto's energy, it helps to get to the core purpose and deep sense of power. The individual will experience new levels of intimacy, not only with herself, but with others, as well, that are uncovered and discovered. There is a great deal of intensity and focus in the life of the individual. With Pluto, there is a probing in deeper things, so that light can be shed on darkness.

As a consequent, this individual will have a chance to evolve and to rebirth, and strip away anything that is unnecessary. A deep experience of the transformational kind will be in the life of this individual, once she accepts it. These are the things that are not working for her, even the thought process. In order for this to happen, there must be a letting go of things that are holding her back from deep and meaningful experiences. Pluto's energy seeks to go somewhere, so I will meet it in guise of events and people. If, for some reason, this individual is attracting jealous, controlling, and manipulative people, then the question that should she should ask is "is there something in myself that it provoking that kind of behavior or circumstance?"

Saturn trine Venus:

There is a chance that this individual knows what is expected of her in personal relationships and by others. Also, this individual is very careful of what is given out or what promises that are made by her, because there is a feeling of obligation to follow through with them. Connections with others are not taken lightly, and she is more attached to long-term committed partnerships, neither is this person a risk taker with the heart. There is a strong sense of responsibility to the ones that this individual loves. This is a natural thing; it is like second nature. It is easy to exercise caution and good judgment in relationships and can be quite understanding when people need it.

One of the things that are important to this individual is that she prides herself in being trustworthy, and would do whatever it takes to be compromising when necessary. It is a part of this individual's nature to help others to climb the ladder of success, even though she had to climb to the top herself. This is one of the main qualities for success in the individual's life; it is the sensitivity to the needs of others. Another quality is that she is a good parent and will be a munificent disciplinarian. There is an expectation for the children to learn how to respect others and be conscious of needs other than their own. In romance, there is a need that there must be respect and loyalty, and only desires a long-term relationship.

Mercury trine Uranus:

When Mercury is trine Uranus, the individual is open to new ideas, and can come up with a unique way of being perspective about the self. There is an interest in computers and a love for technology. The intuition in this individual is very strong, and mostly leads in the right direction. There is a tolerant, friendly and unprejudiced manner about this individual, and will avoid making unfair judgments about people. A very resourceful, witty and quick to grasp new subjects is an attribute to individual, and knows how to be flexible. It can be quite perplexing when others do not think outside of the box, as the individual does.

There is a need for space and freedom to do her own thinking, and does not like when others are trying to force-feed information in any way. These two planets are harmonious when they are in trine, and the individual can experience peace and harmony in her life, and can call upon these traits when needed. There will be a natural flow of using wisdom in expressing the creative self, and this individual will know how to communicate confidently.

Mercury trine Pluto:

This is an important trine with Mercury and Pluto, because it gives the individual the opportunity to go to the root of a problem, once working on it. When communicating, there is a quick and soft spoken force and others will pick up on it captivatingly. There is both a broad range of interest and depth. Indeed, this individual is very adaptable and is a great problem solver. To utilize the acquired skills: the individual needs to spend time analyzing motives; so that a thorough investigation can be done to find out the meaning of life. Once any issues are resolved, there will be a secretive mental energy that will help to free the mind.

Mercury sextile Venus

There are some strong characteristics to this individual's demeanor; she is polite and would know how to choose words carefully, not to offend anyone. The politeness of this individual curtails from a distaste of disharmony and conflict. Because of the desire to please and soothe to keep peace; this individual may not always be direct, which makes it easier to understand others and make a great conversationalist. There is an aim for fairness when dealing with others. Furthermore, there is an appreciation for arts and attempts to achieve balance and harmony in social relationships, personal environment, writing, and speech. This individual will do well in counseling, art, relationships, or design.

Grand mutable cross:

This chart shows that it is a Grand mutable Cross which has four planets in the same modes. It also represents four areas of life. All the planets are connected together, along with four squares and two oppositions. The Grand mutable Cross also has a planet in each element (Earth, Air, Water, & Fire). There is also a combination of squares included, in the Grand mutable Cross. There is a unique expression and interpretation of this cross, because they are stressful structures. The squares motivate action, and can be perceived as uncomfortable influences. If the tension builds up, action would be taken, but depending on the actions that are taken: the squares can either be constructive or destructive.

Consequently, they are hard to ignore, because they offer a solid foundation; and they can be very resourceful. It can be challenging to find the point of assimilation, but the key is to find balance in the oppositions. They would yield the amount of force on the planets creating a solid base. However, when there is no balance, the structure cannot hold up, and there can be some form of frustration on the individual's psyche.

References:

Acker, L., S.; Sakoian, F.; (1973) *The astrologers handbook: With complete instructions for interpreting any natal chart & step by step instructions for casting your own chart. New York, NY Harper & Brow, Publishers, Inc.*

Arroyo, S.; (1993) *Relationships and life cycles: Astrological patterns of personal experience. CRCS Publications.*

Arroyo, S.; (1989) *Chart interpretation handbook: Guidelines for understanding the essentials of the birth chart. CRCS Publications.*

Arroyo, S.; (1975) *Astrology, psychology, and the four elements: An energy approach & its use in the counseling arts. CRCS Publication.*

Bloch, D.; George, D.; (2006) *Astrology for yourself: A workbook for personal transformation: How to understand and interpret your own birth chart. Lake Worth, FL. Nicholas-Hays, Inc.*

Cunningham, D.; (1999) *How to read your astrological chart: Aspects of the cosmic puzzle. York Beach, ME. Red Wheel/Weiser, LLC.*

Goldsmith-Jacobson, I., M.; (1975) *In the beginning astrology. Alhambra, CA. Frank Severy Publishing.*

Greene, L.; Sasportas, H.; (1985) *The twelve houses: An introduction to the houses in astrological interpretation. Hammersmith, London. Mackays of Chatham, PLC.*

Hand, R.; (1981) *Horoscope symbols. Surrey, England. Schiffer Publishing, Ltd.*

Heindel, A., F.; Heindel, M.; (1973) *The message of the stars. Oceanside, CA. The Rosicrucian Fellowship.*

Hickey, I., M.; (1992) *Astrology: A cosmic science. Sebastopol, CA. CRCS Publications.*

Holy Bible *Kings James Version*

Lehman, J., L.; (1996) *Classical astrology fir modern living: from ptolemy to psychology & back again. Atglen, GA. Whitford Press.*

Lehman, J., L.; (1992) *The book of rulerships: Keywords from classical astrology. Westchester, PA. Whitford Press.*

Lehman, J., L.; (1989) *Essential dignities. Westchester, PA. Whitford Press.*

Pelletier, R.; (1978) *Planets in houses. Rockport, MA. R. R Donnelley & Sons Co.*

Pelletier, R.; (1974) *Planes in aspects: Understanding your inner dynamics. Atglen, PA. Para Research, Inc.*

Rudhyar, D.; (1980) *Person centered astrology.*

Rudhyar, D.; (1972) *The astrological houses: The spectrum of individual experience. CRCS Publications.*

Rudhyar, D.; (1970) *The astrology of personality: A re-formulation of astrological concepts and ideals, in terms of contemporary psychology and philosophy.*

Tierney, B.; (1983) *Dynamics of aspects analysis: New perceptions in astrology. CRCS Publications.*